LOVE
Happier

LOVE
Happier

The Art and Practice of Relationship

MAGALI PEYSHA

ZEIG, TUCKER & THEISEN, INC.
PHOENIX, ARIZONA

Copyright 2018 Magali Peysha

All rights reserved under International and Pan-American Copyright Conventions. No part of this book may be reproduced, stored in a retrieval system or transmitted in any form by an electronic, mechanical, photocopying, recording means or otherwise, without prior written permission of the author.

Book design by Maureen Cutajar
www.gopublished.com

Please note that names and identifying characteristics have been changed throughout this book to protect the privacy of individuals. Any resemblance to a known person is purely coincidental.

Library of Congress Cataloging-in-Publication Data

Love Happier The Art and Practice of Relationship
/ Peysha, Magali.—1st edition
p. cm.
Includes bibliographic references

ISBN 978-1-934442-60-9 (pbk : alk paper)

Published by
Zeig, Tucker & Theisen, Inc.
2632 East Thomas Rd., Suite 201
Phoenix, AZ 85016
www.zeigtucker.com

Manufactured in the United States of America

CONTENTS

	Introduction	1
1.	Love Styles	7
2.	How I Want to Feel	25
3.	Love Strengths	33
4.	The Fantastic Five	35
5.	Destructive Patterns	41
6.	Love Modality	45
7.	Creating Greater Connection	49
8.	Our Many Marriages	55
9.	Rules & Jealousy	63
10.	Steps to Prevent Future Jealousy	69
11.	The Disappearing Husband	71
12.	Forgiving Yourself and Each Other	77
13.	Cover Problems	81
14.	Creating Your Mission Statement	87
15.	Money & Love	91

16.	Dating	97
17.	Date Ideas	101
18.	The Kids	105
19.	Passion & Chemistry	109
20.	Presence: The Man Inside	115
21.	Boy and Man	117
22.	Polarity	121
23.	Warrior & Goddess	127
24.	Resistance to Love	131

INTRODUCTION

Being in romantic relationship with another human being is probably one of the bravest things you will ever do. In addition to the good stuff, committed relationships come equipped with doubts, emotions, questions, rules, and desires.

Many people will at some point ask, "What am I doing? Are we just too different to make this work?"

If you and your partner have been together a while, you might wonder, "How do we keep growing our love after so many years?"

And, unfortunately, most of us experience our fair share of pain and hurt along the way. And the pain can sometimes take on the intensity of trauma, which gets reborn when there is disagreement or stress. This pattern usually leads to regret about the choices we've made.

My guess is that even with all this uncertainty you also have some very powerful reasons for wanting to be in relationship and wanting more from love — and that wanting more has led to some big questions.

How do I get the spark back?

What does it take to be happy together for the long haul?

How can we communicate in a more loving way?

All of us have asked such questions. And most of us have seen couples who seem to have this longed-for chemistry, commitment, and trust. What we don't know is what these couples do to keep their love growing, to keep it evolving.

If you're reading this book, I know that's the piece that has your attention, it is a big part of what you want for yourself and your partner.

And just the fact that you are reading these words shows me that you're ready to take action to make a positive difference in your relationship.

Truthfully, creating the space in which an ongoing and deepening love can be nurtured starts with this simple decision to grow yourself, to practice new skills, and to take a few brave steps.

And in this book, I want to show you that you can have more love in your life than you may have ever believed possible.

I also want to show you that no matter how long you've been in a relationship, there are always ways to grow the love and to discover new things about one another.

Even if you have been married for 30 years and wonder if it is really possible to change ...

Even if you're in a brand-new relationship and want to start off on the right foot — growing together, and understanding each other more fully...

Even if you are totally new to love and have never felt those first butterflies in your stomach when thinking about, or being in the presence of, the other ...

This book will fill in all those blanks and others!

And I believe this with all my heart because I know what it's like to really invest in your relationship — your emotions, mind, and spirit. My husband Mark and I have been married for 25 years and have been committed to each other for 30 years. And even though we met at 18 years old, our love has evolved so many times over those years that, with each new layer, a deeper belief builds inside of me that rejuvenation of love is possible for every couple.

Why do I believe this so strongly?

Because I've worked with thousands of couples. And I will teach you how by taking small action steps forward each day your love can be activated or reactivated.

And that's the journey we're going to take together. We will establish our map with the "10 Love Styles."

In the first chapter, we're going to explore the 10 different Love Styles so that you will be able to tailor your steps to be the most effective possible.

- With the assessment we provide, you will be able to determine your own top three Love Styles, so that you can gain deeper insight into what love means for you.
- A great benefit is that you can invite your partner to take the quiz as well. This way you can figure out what makes your relationship tick — both its good aspects and those that might be marked with "room-for-improvement."
- Together, we are going to search for your individual secrets, patterns, and needs — and your lover's individual needs, desires, and patterns.

After establishing your Love Styles, you are going to explore your relationship using fresh understanding and action-taking as your compass. By the way, your lover doesn't even need to read this book — he or she will feel a difference in you and the relationship you share. Through the actions suggested and the discoveries made, you will build a whole new way of loving each other. Most important, love itself will take on an entirely new dimension.

Much of what I describe in this book about love has been influenced by the couples I've coached. As I teach, Passion Patterns Coaching to Coaches (numbering in the thousands), I always learn more and more. No two relationships are alike, and I am lucky to hear from individuals and couples almost daily about how my Passion Pattern strategies are working in their lives, with clients, and often with spouses.

Truthfully, it is the feedback from clients that has led to the creation of this book — and to all the strategies that I talk about in its chapters, including how to cope with challenges like jealousy, negative patterns, intimacy, energy, money issues, and parenting.

But love isn't only about challenges. I provide lots of strategies to spice things up: infusing your dates with more creativity and romance, enhancing your intimate side, and showing appreciation and love for your partner in the style that he or she can best receive.

On the other side of challenge there is opportunity. Thus, our exploration will encompass ways to support new positive relational habits. For example:

- You'll learn how to find out what your partner really wants to feel, and how to connect at that level.
- You'll discover your own love strengths and how best to use them, and you'll get to identify the ways that work best for you to express your unique love. You'll explore how to appreciate your partner — and be appreciated in return.
- You'll create your own definitions of forgiveness and trust, which means finally being able to free yourself from the tricky memories or fears that hold you back.
- You'll learn how to cope when there are disagreements about money, parenting, and other big life issues, and you'll find out how to use these moments to make your relationship stronger.
- You'll find a thousand ways (outlined here and invoked) to rekindle the sparks of intimacy and passion every single day.

The benefits you gain from this book will last long after you close it. As you enlist the strategies to help you navigate the ups and downs of your relationship — and to deepen and sweeten your love — the richness of your evolving life together will affect you and everyone around you.

And if you work with couples, the strategies and the stories of real-life couples I've coached will motivate, inspire, and get you thinking and working at an even higher level of relationship support.

By the way, for all of you coaches, I suggest you try everything out first. This way, when you suggest a strategy or action to a client, you will get to know firsthand how it can benefit him or her. After all, our own relationships are our greatest teachers. The work we do in the world has a profound effect on our own hearts and how we experience love. What we discover on the path with our partner will shape our work with our clients.

How you grow in your personal and professional relationships is a journey that invariably affects your experience of joy, connection, and growth in your life. I am thrilled to be part of the journey with you and look forward to hearing from you and perhaps even meeting you one day. You will hear me mention the Passion Patterns training throughout the chapters. This is a course Mark and I teach to couples and to Relationship Coaches. Much of what I am teaching you in this book has evolved in real time as I have helped people in training to expand their relationships. In other words, the text is infused with the practical wisdom that can only emerge from collaborating with real people facing real challenges and discovering real solutions!

CHAPTER 1

Love Styles

Let's first talk about what we mean by a Love Style. What exactly is it? And how can it help you make your relationship more loving, trusting, exciting, and intimate?

Once you know your style — and your partner's style — you will have a better understanding of how your love works. You will see the ways in which you are unique and also very similar to other people who have the same style.

And you can feel good knowing that even if your Love Style is different from your partner's style, it's okay, and even essential! You don't have to have the same Love Styles — in fact, similarity can sometimes work against you! The key is getting to really know your partner's patterns and needs, and accepting that there are many different ways to experience love. Once this understanding is in place,, more room is created for greater freedom and growth in your relationship. Knowing your Love Style and that of your partner is more important than any cultural ideas of what being in love means, or notions of how to be "good" in relationship, or any of the so-called "secrets" of successful couples. Understanding Love Styles gives you a window into the real secrets and rewards of being in relationship with your lover, soul mate, and life partner.

The Love Styles Quiz

Have you ever wondered why a friend has such an easy time flirting with her husband of 14 years? Or why someone else seems to be able to resolve painful disagreements easily, when you would be either muttering curses under your breath or crying into a pillow, or doing both? Our Relationship Styles are just as unique, unplanned, and important as our personalities. I'd argue they are even more important to explore because a lot less attention is given to Relationship Styles. I'd like to change that right now with the Love Styles Quiz.

But before you take the quiz, know that you probably fit more than one type or style — most of us are a combination of two or even more Love Styles. You might even be a new Love Style all together, a combination of three or four styles that emerge as something new. Now it's true that all of us are unique, but identifying our tendencies helps us learn how to mix more effectively and with greater ease with our partner's style.

Well, it's time to take the Love Styles Quiz. Just go to LoveStylesQuiz.com. The quiz will take about 10-20 minutes to complete. Please be as honest as possible in your answers, as that will give you the most accurate results when it comes to your top 3 Love Styles, and following the tips and exercises in the rest of the book.

Once you have your results, you can read the rest of this chapter with a specific focus on your own Love Styles — and those of your partner.

If your partner is willing to take the quiz, great! If not, you can read about the different styles here and probably make a pretty educated guess about which ones apply.

While it's important to focus on the Love Styles that are relevant to you, I do recommend reading about all the different Love Styles. All of them may have something for you in terms of understanding both what is specifically relevant and the spectrum of possibility. Everything in perspective.

Welcome back! Now we're going to go through each of the different styles in detail, so you can better grasp your results. First, here's the list of Love Styles.

The Love Styles

1. Playful and Light
2. Sex Goddess/God
3. Earthy, Steady & Grounded
4. Creative & Surprising
5. Driven & Goal Oriented
6. Inner Geek
7. Best Friend
8. Knight in Shining Armor
9. Escape With Me
10. Commune of Love

Now, let's look at each one to review its characteristics and some of the elements to consider when one style crosses paths with other styles.

Love Style #1 — Playful and Light

"The good pirate enjoys a chase."

Full of energy, good vibes, and good times.

Playful and light lovers are focused on enjoying the moment, being spontaneous, and spreading positive energy to others.

At times, you may feel that a romantic partner brings your mood down because he or she lacks your energy and zest for life.

You love to surprise the woman or man in your life, whether with a new trampoline, a trip to an exotic locale to play with dolphins, or a visit to an unusual local neighborhood to sample the possibilities. Fun in love is easy because everything is about energy, the joy of the moment, and feeling good.

You have a lot of empathy, but you need to bring others emotions up. If you can't improve your partner's mood to meet yours, then you may take this as a sign that the relationship isn't working and decide to look for another partner.

When someone is critical of you, you might try to detach because the person's emotions turn you off and bring you down. And seeing the good in so many people can make it hard to commit to only one.

Your lover may not be able to keep up with you, which might create a feeling that the relationship "wasn't meant to be." Of course, you will continue to be friends after the intimate relationship is over. Hard feelings aren't part of your vocabulary either.

You acknowledge that there is sometimes the need for serious work but it never seems to be the priority. Why put off feeling good? That makes no sense to you when you can feel good right now.

Meet Lisa and Jeremy

Imagine that Lisa is a playful and light lover who seeks out a partner who is naturally more serious, like Jeremy. Lisa enjoys making Jeremy laugh and smile. And while Jeremy tries to be more lighthearted for a while, after 6 months or so he falls back into his old more sober ways. But now Jeremy expects Lisa to be his mood-lifter all the time…and he complains that Lisa doesn't understand his more serious side.

"Love and relationship can't be all fun and games," Jeremy thinks. So what was initially attractive now works against Lisa. In this situation, growth and understanding are needed. When Lisa, the playful one, learns more about Jeremy's moodiness, she can find different ways to show love. She can find ways that are not just about enhancing his mood. This expansion in perspective helps her to grow with Jeremy, and this means that Jeremy doesn't just have to "keep up" with Lisa. Lisa and Jeremy can find activities that bring out excitement and depth, which they both crave in their own ways.

Love Style #2 — Sex Goddess/God
"Passion Rules"

Nothing is as good as intimacy and physical connection.

You might be an intellectual, an artist, or a change maker, but you know that what you really are is a lover. Whether you've called yourself a sex addict, or you're in a committed relationship, or you're a serial monogamist, you love the physical pleasures of love over all other forms of intimacy.

Your passionate nature means you are always ready, and sex is usually on your mind. You can be frustrated by a partner's style not matching yours. You might question whether you are in balance because others lack your sexual appetites.

This style has its downsides. The first is that your needs seem to be too much for one lover. You tire out your man or woman.

You use sex to change your state and haven't learned other ways to make yourself or your lover feel connection.

Friends and family may seem less important to you than your partner, so at times you feel overly dependent on him or her. The intense emotions that lead to passionate connection can also turn into anger, jealousy, and vengeance.

Learning to satisfy a partner who has different needs for connection can feel frustrating because it is hard work.

However, when you do understand that your lover needs different sources of intimacy and that you can satisfy him or her on levels other than physical passion, not only will you come into better balance, you will also deepen the intimate and passionate connection between you and your lover.

Meet Patrick

In Patrick's experience of love he was on a constant roller coaster, going from one great partner to the next. When he did decide to end the ride and get serious, he would feel inauthentic. This sense of not being his true self came from his belief that to be a mature and committed partner he needed to lower his sex drive and needs. Through coaching, Patrick learned to communicate his desire in a way that made his partner feel appreciated and wanted. This was the key.

In the past, when Patrick felt that a lover wasn't enough like him, he would criticize his partner, who would then become defensive. Through using Passion Patterns daily Patrick was able to communicate in a loving way, which elevated his lover. This meant spending much more time enjoying his partner's Love Style. Patrick needed to learn to put himself in his lover's shoes and understand her needs on an emotional and communication level. Then she naturally wanted to understand him better and he could be honest about his fears of needing too much intimacy and sex.

Most adults who are the Sex Goddess/God type of lover reach a point of maturity when they do want to take their sexual love into a committed relationship. Like everyone else, they have fears and doubts about themselves and their appetites. If you're a Sex Goddess/God, it's helpful to understand your other top Love Styles too. You can develop more of your emotional style while staying true to your authentic passion in the area of intimacy. This will give your partner more ways to connect with you and create greater connection in and out of the bedroom.

Love Style #3 — Earthy, Steady & Grounded

"You can count on me."

Consistent, reliable, and connected.
 Feeling connected to what matters most in life comes easy for you. Showing others that you are there for them takes no effort. Whether you're a man or a woman, your consistency of love and

support creates an emotional net that catches the ones you love, cushioning them softly as they approach the Earth.

Back on land, you create consistent energy that gives that special person the ability to soar, to be authentic and natural, and to feel understood.

Challenges may arise when you don't understand the need for change, excitement, or creativity. "Isn't it enough to be together?" you might ask. The relationship is enough for you. You know your emotions, and you're steady in them.

This means that if your lover leaves you, then you take a long time to recover. On the positive side, your consistency makes for life-long relationships. The search for the right person is less appealing than the life you create together.

To grow, you'll need to learn new ways of fulfilling your lover. This may include everything from finding stimulating topics to discuss, embarking on different adventures, exploring new techniques in the bedroom, to delving more deeply into the modality through which your partner experiences love most directly, such as touch, speech, sight, sound, or energy.

Meet Marissi and Ben

When Marissi came to the Passion Patterns training she was in a tough spot. Her husband was tired of her unwillingness to explore new experiences in their relationship. Marissi had a big breakthrough in her first class. She realized that she wasn't bad or wrong, she was just very different from her husband.

By the third week, Marissi had started to surprise her husband in small ways that were fun. Before the training she had thought everything he wanted was really hard to do and would involve too much change, but she soon learned that small changes could be powerful. Her daily question became, "How will I surprise Ben?" She might get him a gift or a arrange a surprise date, and she even learned to speak to him in a sexy new voice. This last change surprised her the most. It was actually a voice she had used 20 years earlier when they first met. Marissi's husband had been telling her for years that he craved more adventure in life.

Until now she had thought it wasn't within her domain as his wife to add that to their relationship. So her response was to suggest he go on outdoor adventures or take up new hobbies. When instead she took action to bring small daily adventures into their interactions, her husband was thrilled. This led to him wanting to understand her needs on a new level.

Love Style #4 — Creative & Surprising

"Don't bore me."

Life is a mystery and there is magic to be discovered.

Have you ever wondered why life is never boring for you? Endless opportunities await your attention. Whether you are learning a new technical skill, painting your bedroom, or traveling off to Burning Man, life is an ever-evolving journey. You look for a partner who will express the same joy and adventure you crave.

Love is more than emotional; it is also action, spirit, and transformation. You live to do, imagine, and create. You look for a soul mate who appreciates your nature, respects your work, and enjoys your vision.

When not at your best, you may be moody, hard to understand, and unclear. What you seek is hard to express in words. If your partner is more on the logical side, then you may feel misunderstood or undervalued. Your relationship, like your life, must be a work of art that you co-create.

Life sometimes gets in the way of your love when circumstances change. For example, a new stage may be beginning with the birth of a child or a job promotion so that life suddenly becomes more intense. Or the physical body changes, and once-simple tasks become more difficult. These are the moments when you will need to adapt and create different sorts of adventure for the two of you.

It is in your nature to seek excitement, so with maturity will come fresh opportunities — as long as you are flexible enough to let go of the previous stage of life and embrace the new.

I was speaking with my good friend Keith one day and he asked me, "Magali, why do I always date women who are so different from me?" As we went deeper into his inquiry we discovered that Keith had a limiting belief, which was camouflaged in a strength. Keith believed that his Love Style of being creative and surprising was a strength. However, when it came to dating he tended to meet and commit to women who were a lot more stable and even a bit boring to him. He had been operating from the belief that you look for the opposite in your partner to create a solid match — opposites attract, right?

The problem was that Keith could never stay in the relationship. After a time, he felt that his girlfriends only wanted him to be a "husband," or "father." While Keith craved another creative spirit to dance through life with, he also believed that women who were like him would be his undoing, that they'd drive him mad with jealousy or drama. This belief was based on an experience with a college girlfriend who had been a bit eccentric and left him with a broken heart. His conclusion was that he should find the opposite type of women.

Through understanding that he could change his belief and forge a more empowering belief, Keith opened his eyes to all the women he already knew who shared his same zest for living. Until this point, he had friend-zoned women who shared his creative spirit. Soon Keith began to date a good friend who shared his same Love Style.

Some people really flourish when they find a partner who has a similar Love Style. And a partner may have the same Love Style but be different in other areas of life. For example, a committed stay-at-home mom or dad might marry a person who is passionate about work. However, both may value creativity and passion for their "day jobs." Perhaps they also love to make their holidays and weekends dynamic and filled with innovative expression. So, on the surface the one who is dedicated to raising kids and the one who is dedicated to career seem different, but beneath the surface they share a way of being. Once this is revealed, the couple will feel a greater sense of unity and power together.

Love Style #5 — Driven & Goal Oriented

"We can conquer all."

Everything is possible if we put our minds to it.

A relationship has goals, achievements, and rules. You know what you want, and you want a person who knows what he or she wants too. To succeed means to plan, do, and strategize.

The goal-oriented lover is smart, decisive, and driven. You may know exactly how you want your relationship to work. You want your partner to share your vision. Growth for your relationship may involve greater flexibility and communication.

The relationship is another area of life you want to achieve in, and this can mean great lovemaking. You will not settle for less than great.

A possible downside is that you focus on the future, forgetting to experience the present moment and the desires and needs of your partner. You may focus too much on work and think your partner should understand that all your hard work is done to achieve a future goal together.

Keeping communication open and emotional can be a challenge for you. To grow and deepen love, you will need to learn more about your lover's feelings as well as your own.

Finding ways to enjoy the present and using planning and foresight to create joy for the two of you can be a good choice in this case.

Meet Mindy and Tom

Mindy and Tom were struggling in their marriage. Eventually, Mindy was able to convince Tom to try Passion Patterns training.

What surprised them both was that Tom was good at applying lessons and directives. He actually took the course in a competitive spirit, very in line with his Love Style. Mindy was thrilled. Tom saw that the patterns were something he could do, and this enabled him to drop his defensive and righteous attitude. Now, the couple goes on weekly dates, and Tom consistently asks Mindy to share for ten minutes straight about her day and her feelings. Mindy feels so understood that she no longer minds Tom's intense schedule and energy. Instead she feels lucky to have such a fiery and directed husband.

Love Style #6 — Inner Geek

"Do you really get me?"

Geeking out together.

Whether it is reading, gaming, or technology, you like details and facts. When it comes to your partner, you love all of his or her interests and abilities, but sometimes you forget to ask, "How are you?"

It is easy for you to find stimulating topics of conversations and hold strong opinions. You have a tendency to mate for life and be a loyal and caring lover.

On the other hand, you might miss emotional cues and forget about the other's perspective. It helps you to be with a grounded earthy type who, like you, is loyal.

But, unlike you, the grounded earthy type can provide nurturing balance and presence. When you are confronted by the chaos of love, you may get disoriented and run for the imaginary hills of your favorite sci-fi book, movie, or game.

You might think this type is all about being young and immature. However, I meet this client often, and find that they tend to be mature and work in technology, engineering, or academia.

They often feel misunderstood because they love so much and give so much, but their partners don't seem to get it. Also, they often know they are turning to escapism, but they are sure that this is better than leaving the relationship or getting angry.

Escapism is a relief valve. What they are missing is an understanding of how to love in a more complete way and the accompanying insights into what a partner needs in order to really feel loved. For this reason, it is really important to think of your partner as a puzzle that you must figure out. Create a goal that says, "I will understand more about my partner each day!"

Meet Justin

I was coaching a man named Justin, who immediately saw that he had the Inner Geek Love Style. Once he saw this, he admitted that he had no idea how to change to be more compatible with his wife, who was a coach. Justin had developed an identity around not being good with real people and not being good enough in relationship. He repeated often that he had no idea why his wife loved him so much.

It was important for Justin to understand, on both a head and heart level, why his wife loved him. He needed to know his strengths as well as his weaknesses (such as the weakness of escaping into games and books). Once Justin felt more empowered as a lover, he could then begin to take action in real time with his wife. Before working with me, he had always thought that if he wanted to please his wife, he would have to become a different person. However, he learned that there were simple adjustments he could make that would create big changes: for example, by just listening to her for a few minutes with full attention first thing in the morning and at the end of the day, she began to feel more loved. It surprised Justin to learn that she had always felt second-best to his hobbies and interests. He remedied this by reminding her daily that she was first in his life. This relaxed a lot of painful tension between the two of them.

Very quickly Justin and his wife were doing more activities together, some of which Justin previously had assumed she would find boring. Justin also became much more comfortable in himself, and this led to a big improvement in their intimate life.

Love Style #7 — Best Friend
"I've got your back, babe."

Clear, Calm, and Certain.

For you, being in love also means being similar. You choose a mate who shares your tendencies, likes, and aesthetics. It is hard to imagine that others wouldn't want a best friend as a life partner.

Harmony is a normal part of a relationship, you think. Fights are not easy or necessary. You know how to get along with others, and you know how to share your feelings.

Your partner is your first priority even if you have many friends. You are likely to tell your lover that he or she is also your best friend. You may even fall in love with your best friend.

One downside to this style may be that your relationship could become a little predictable. Since you don't like disagreement or to rock the boat, you tend not to admit your feelings — even to yourself. Thus, when your partner broaches a sensitive topic, you are shocked.

Watch out not to be a rescuer; this could lead to being with someone because of a sense of obligation instead of being drawn by love and passion.

Best friends do make the best of lovers, as long as you work to keep the flame of passion ignited and don't begin to believe that friendship is enough. This can sometimes happen to best friend types because they value that part of the relationship so highly.

Meet Maria

Maria had met her husband when she was 18 years old. They were married by 20. Now, some 20 years later, she was feeling that the relationship lacked passion. I asked her how long she had felt this way and she answered about 19 years. Actually, this isn't unusual. Most couples go through a honeymoon phase of six months to three years and then they settle into whatever patterns emerge after the excitement has worn off.

Maria felt completely committed but often sad and stuck because she had no idea how to flirt or invite romance back into the relationship. The first step for Maria was to acknowledge her desires for greater chemistry. Finally.

The next step was to be very clear with her husband about how excited she was about allowing herself to feel sexy. Maria didn't need much more than this clarity and a way to ask her husband for his help. Instead of the typical mistake of complaining to him that he didn't make her feel sexy, she owned her desire to be sexy and asked for support. Her husband was more than happy to help her. Through understanding that she was married to a best friend (with a strong secondary rescue style), Maria and I made use of the husband's natural tendency to be the helper. Without ever even coming to coaching, her husband was empowered to support her desire. Naturally, he too became a lot sexier in her eyes.

Love Style #8 — Knight in Shining Armor

"Here to save the day."

There's a Solution to Every Problem.

No matter what the predicament is, you will find a solution or new way to see things that makes it better. You'll rescue the lover who needs you. Being needed feels so good.

You not only enjoy being needed and appreciated, you feel it is a core part of you. How you give is how you love. When your lover struggles, you are by his or her side, no question.

But when your lover becomes independent, you feel challenged and unsure of the relationship. You might look for a person outside of the relationship to rescue. This might take the form of a friendship or a charity, but it could even lead to an affair.

The first possible downside is that you find yourself wanting to save more than one person. Your spouse may become jealous of your tendency to rescue others and the energy you spend taking care of everyone else. (Although, of course, your partner may love this instinct in you too.)

Make sure that you work hard to let your partner know that he or she is number one. Grow by learning that a partner can need you and be independent both. Learn to experience your partner's love in many different ways and through his or her different emotions.

Start to make a point of seeing and recognizing independence, and even if it is scary, let your partner know how happy it makes you to see these shifts. Noticing positive independence is the first step to appreciating it.

And, a bonus: intimacy can be especially fun when you open up to your creative masculine or feminine side and allow role-playing to be a part of your lovemaking. You may want to bring the rescuer into the bedroom in a fun and passionate way. Or, you may want to highlight that independent spirit.

Most of the people I know who are rescuers are quite blind to this Love Style. Only when it leads to an affair do they take notice and want to create a shift in themselves.

A rescuer benefits from clarity about priorities in their relationships. They need to recognize the positive parts of their style, as well as to be able to identify when they are going too far into rescue mode. Rescuers can get so swept up in the rescue that their priorities go topsy turvy. Usually, the priority in one's life is the spouse and children, and then extended family, followed by friends, and then community. This order, however, can get turned around for rescuers.

So, get it down on paper and begin with a goal of clarifying your true priorities — and showing your partner that he or she is number one. This might mean taking time away from rescue mode in the community or with friends. Remember, your relationship may at times be in need of rescue — even if your partner is successful in his or her own life.

Love Style #9 — Escape with Me

"We can forget the world together."

Sailing Away to the Land of…

Loving is lovely, especially when you get to forget about the world together. Think of the lyrics to the Jack Johnson song: "Making banana pancakes, pretend that it's the weekend, now, we can pretend it all the time." Two people who share this style might find it hard to get much done, but they will have a hell of a lot of fun anyway.

You have the ability to make your sweetheart feel that he or she is the best person in the world. When you create your world together, it is cozy, sweet, and full of your unique spirit. You've probably been called a romantic.

You know I'm talking to you: the boy or girl who watched that movie 10 times because the main characters were just so perfect and their fate so doomed.

You can make a loving relationship your oasis. Just stop imagining one and make a real relationship happen.

When out of balance, you become unsure of yourself and your choices. If you don't get enough time away from the world, you have a tendency to burn out.

You will turn to your partner for rescue, and if he or she isn't the rescuing sort, then it can be a challenge to build your own raft.

Find a way to give to yourself at the spirit level every day so that you never get desperate enough to run away all together — from your life or partner. For you, imagination and creativity and time to just be are essential. This means planning healthy breaks from the world. If your partner doesn't understand this need, it is your job to ask for his or her help. Oftentimes we forget that the other person can be truly helpful and might have greater insights than we do!

So, go ahead and ask your partner to tell you when and how this part of you, the "let's run away together" part, is most appealing. Plan weekend getaways with your lover. See if there are ways that he or she would like to be included in your daily or weekly breaks from the world. Most people are drawn to this powerful style because they also need those breaks from the status quo on some level, but they are not as good as you are at creating the right tone or making the time. This realization means becoming a strategic leader that brings your Love Style to your partner's experience instead of escaping the relationship in order to accommodate it somehow.

Love Style #10 — Commune of Love

"The more the merrier."

Love Is To Be Shared.

"The more the merrier" may be your motto. Let's go to the party! Or throw the party! Or find the party! As long as there are people, you're happy. And you're extra happy when everyone's together. You may feel your best when surrounded by friends and family. It's a given you assume that if someone loves you he or she also will love the people you love.

But what happens when your partner doesn't agree with you? It can be a challenge for you to see another perspective. It can be difficult to believe, for example, that a dear friend is not nice to your partner, and so your partner doesn't want to spend time with this friend. Being able to step back and see things from other perspectives is essential to your relationship skills.

If you waited a long time to find your significant other, then you already have your crowd of people who love you, and it can be a challenge to integrate a new person into that crowd. Also, always relating to the "crowd" may foster feelings of jealousy and possessiveness in your lover.

Try to keep as organized as you can with your "party" schedule and always invite your partner to the events. When you're at an event, show your friends that your partner is your priority, and once your partner feels secure in that place, he or she will likely laugh and dance the night away by your side.

Like all Love Styles, this one is hard to see in oneself because it feels so natural and right to be this way. So, if you are wondering, "Is this me?" Then take a look at what boyfriends, girlfriends, or spouses have said to you in the past or what they find confusing now. Do they complain that you don't do enough with them alone? Do they complain that they feel left out of your friend life, or family life? If a partner reports such feelings, it may be time to set some new priorities.

Try visualizing yourself and your partner in the middle of all your friends and social engagements. Imagine how it will be to have that one special person with you more often. What will he or she need to feel good when with you in a social space? Then check out what the other person's Love Style is. How can you honor the style and make it a priority to give to your partner through his or her Love Style. Perhaps you will need to dedicate half the weekend to the other's style and half to yours. Remember to tell your partner that you recognize how much your social life has taken center stage. Explain that you want to include him or her and also honor his or her Love Style. This shift in attention will be a big game changer.

PUTTING IT ALL TOGETHER

Now that we've covered all of the different *Love Styles*, you probably have a better idea of what it means to be in a relationship that encompasses both your style(s) and your partner's style(s).

Awareness is half the journey and it's also a resource to find the directions in that journey. We're going to use awareness to foresee potential pitfalls in your relationship, taking a closer look at conflicts that might arise from a difference in Love Styles, and looking at simple ways to bring you and your partner closer together. Let's energize your love life by adding new patterns of connection, communication, and love —every step of the way.

CHAPTER 2

How I Want to Feel

Have you ever asked yourself, "How can I be happier in my relationship?" So often we want more, without having any idea how to create the love, trust, and passion that seems as if it should just come naturally. People often fall into a trap of expecting love to flow continuously, easily, almost magically. I believe that whoever you are inside, a part of you wants to give love and receive love. And once you break through your fears, you will discover the trust, intimacy, and connection you may not have known were possible. The following chapters will answer some of your key questions, and provide the tools to make your love dynamic and intimate.

First, I want to congratulate you for taking the time to really improve your relationship. As you already have guessed, each chapter is designed to help you learn a new relationship strength, understand yourself better, and take action in your day-to-day life. Next, you are going to learn how to prioritize, communicate, give, and receive at a whole new level. You will find yourself opening up to deeper purpose and trust, greater intimacy, and, yes, more and more love.

In addition to insights and observations, you'll find a host of questions to ask yourself as you take in the guidance you need to work through the exercises in each chapter. Take time between chapters to put the strategies into practice. Reading is one thing, but it's taking action — applying all the a-ha's — that will make the difference.

A potent goal is to begin having a daily glimpse of love in your relationship. Just a minute each day spent noticing something new, and taking fresh action — internal or external, through words, thoughts, or feelings — will get you on your way to building up your relationship super powers.

I Wish My Relationship Were....

We all have a heartfelt desire to enjoy ourselves in a relationship. We crave fulfillment, growth, connection, and excitement. This is why we seek out love, and I'm guessing this is why you are reading this book — you are hoping to find the path to a better relationship. We all have different parts of our relationship we wish to improve or change, and the best place to begin is with you.

What Do You Want, Really?

So let's start with what you want. Often, there's a tendency to focus on how we want our partner to treat us: I want him to be more present, more supportive, more romantic. I want her to be sexy, to be there for me instead of for everyone else, to be more positive.

Everyone has a private want list, and that's okay, but right now I'd like you to take that list and archive it in the dustiest, most boring and isolated part of your own personal library — the section called "memory."

Now, let's leave that part of this sphere together and move into a place you love. Perhaps this place is working alongside others, or at a busy restaurant, or with a few close friends in a quiet park, or in the cozy corner of your favorite room where you like to read. When you enter this feel-good place, you may feel relaxed or maybe charged up, ambitious, and excited. Are you at home? Are you at work? Are you in a place of learning? Take a minute to find this special place. Close your eyes and be there. Smell it. Listen to it. Feel it. See it. So, you are there — and I'm there with you.

Now Let yourself think about how you like to feel when you are with your partner. Tell yourself how you want to feel.

Write it down:

I want to feel ...
I want to feel ...
I want to feel ...

Go ahead and make a list right now of some of the desired feelings. Let your mind wander: How do you want to feel?

Don't worry, two of your ways may seem to contradict each other — I want to feel peaceful and excited — that's okay. List as many ways as you can: playful, intense, loving, sexy, protective, beautiful, attractive, funny. These feelings are your guide, your motivation, your map. And they keep you focused on the present and the future — what can be — instead of the past and what has been. As you look at the what you have written, you might notice some sentences like this: "I never want to feel lonely," or "I hate feeling jealous or confused." Just draw a line through these sentences. Hit archive. It may help to rewrite those sentences with the future in mind rather than the past. So, if you wrote, "I never want to feel jealous," you change it to read, "I want to feel secure," or "I want to know I'm protected." Do you feel the difference?

Together we are creating a map of where you're going (you already know where you've been), changing the lens on your emotions, inviting the feelings you'll soon get to experience, the relationship you will soon have, and the new understandings that will take you through your day and night with enthusiasm. For this we need a really strong map. And your map is drawn from how you want to feel. So moving from how you don't want to feel, to how you do want to feel sets a good direction. We move towards the good feeling and not just away from the bad one.

If you have only one or two or three feelings written down, then I want you to go back to the place you feel most like you in. You can use this landscape whenever you need to find your authentic heart self. Envisioning a metaphorical place to go to whenever you want allows you to access your authentic state as a person — and as a partner. Now, if you haven't already done it, stop reading, and write all the ways you want to feel with your partner down.

Make sure you have come up with a big, exciting list of feelings.

Now look at this list and pick the top 4 to 7 feelings. All the feelings are good, but these are the ones you need to have all the time. These are both fuel and purpose.

Now, for each of these feelings, write down something you can do with your lover, something you can say to your lover, some way you can surprise your lover, something you can give to your lover that will actually provide you with the feeling you identified as being so important. You are actively taking control of creating these feelings inside yourself.

For example, let's say the feeling you want is protection? How can you remind the person in a loving way that you crave his or her protection? Could you say, "I'd love you to let me know that you have my back"? Maybe you could say, "A hug would make my day," or make a request, "Give me a hug." Maybe it's more like, "Remind me why I started this project at work, that's now driving me nuts." Or, at the end of a long day, "Remind me what I love about parenting, even on a day like today."

The goal here is to feel protected and you're teaching your partner exactly what you need to help you feel this way. Your partner isn't learning how to be a mindreader (wishful thinking is dangerous). You are learning how to be honest, bold, trusting, and deeply loving in your communication and in the energy you share with your partner. In this process, you are giving your partner ways to show his or her love, providing the tools needed to get through to you.

Be honest though, you're not always the easiest person to give to! Sometimes we get in our own way and make it hard for the people who love us the most to give us what we need. This is how we protect ourselves from being vulnerable and getting hurt.

Unfortunately, most couples tend to "ask" for what they want by complaining about what they don't have. If they are mature and great at communicating, they will instead invite a heartfelt discussion of what is wrong and needs improvement. In some cases, pretty rarely though, this can work, provided both people are non-defensive. Most of the time, however, these types of discussions end up releasing a big dam of bad feelings and experiences. One or both people in the relationship end up feeling overwhelmed, angry, and hurt.

By approaching our desired emotions in a positive, proactive way, we avoid this cycle, and instead focus on actions that you can take starting today.

When you are doing this activity with your partner:
If you're doing this activity with your partner, trade lists and then for each stated wish, ask: How can I help you feel ...? If the person wants to be sexy or smart, for example, then ask: "How can I help you feel sexy?" "How can I help you feel smart?"

Whatever's on your partner's list is golden. New productive questions can initiate fresh conversation: "When do you most naturally feel this way?" "How often do you want to feel this way?" And if your partner has just given you a look that says, "I don't know," then be patient, and take the opportunity to reassure him or her that you'll find a way. This is what you want your lover to feel, all this good stuff that is specific.

Be honest with yourself and with your lover. It's okay if what you want is to sometimes feel sad, or angry, or full of fire. Tell your partner how he or she can help you feel this in the best possible way, in the way that gives energy not causes guilt. All feelings are perfect here. They are all precious flowers that will grow with your patience and your unrelenting desire to discover more and to give more to each other.

Understanding the other's perspective...

One of the keys to success in a relationship is that when you're giving to your partner, you must get out of your own head, your own preferences, your own prejudices, and your own tastes. All of us have filters that we use to sort out the things that are meaningful in our lives from those that are not. When we perceive something, we go through an unconscious process of classifying whether or not it is right for us, important to us, interesting to us, or something we want to do. It's how the brain works.

Now, when a partner says what he or she wants and needs, in all of its amazing specificity, we tend to filter what we hear, we change what we hear, and sometimes we even dismiss what we hear. We say, "Well, that doesn't make sense to me," and then we stop paying attention or turn off.

For instance, in a relationship, sometimes your partner will share feelings or experiences about which he or she is not proud, perhaps fears or insecurities. What you don't want to do in that moment is say, "Well, it makes no sense to be afraid of that. Let's move on to the next topic." If you do that, then you're judging the person's experience, diminishing his or her natural feelings, instead of empathizing, accepting, and understanding. Your partner wanted you to listen, understand, and offer reassurance, and instead you rejected the communication. Don't worry if this has been a pattern until now, doing the Passion Patterns actively will get you going on new ways of creating love.

As another example, your partner has likes and dislikes that are very specific. She loves paying the bills but hates talking about the savings. He loves following the news, but he has strong political opinions that he can't help but voice. She loves watching tennis, but only when her player wins. He loves walking the dog but not feeding him or cleaning up after him. These are specific tastes, desires, and needs. Simply judging them prevents any further understanding. Instead, getting more details will help you understand the preferences better, what's behind them.

So if your partner shares the list with you — whether based on reading this book or something else — remind yourself that its content is meaningful to him or her, whether or not you understand it or agree with it.

Say to yourself: This is not my list. I'm here for my partner now; this is not about my personal filter. I'm going to lay aside my personal tastes and biases, and I'm here to record and remember yours. I'm here to collect the precious flowers of my lover's preferences, so I can give them to him or her exactly as needed. I'm cultivating a new level of listening and understanding. And I'm savoring these preferences, enjoying how different they are from mine, and appreciating how precious they are to my partner.

A no-judgment attitude allows for greater ease in exploring your partner's needs and preferences for what they really are rather than shutting down.

If you have read this far, engaged with the exercises and ideas offered, you are already getting to know yourself and your partner better. The next chapters will be about how you give and how you receive so that you get to feel more and feel better all the time. Your relationship deserves to have this baseline of understanding, emotional freedom, and trust. You deserve to know how to make your partner feel the way he or she wants to feel. Taking the chance to really understand the other's needs obviously benefits that person — and it also benefits you. The relationship can be a richer, more energized place to be.

And it doesn't matter if you're different from one another. In fact, it's probably more exciting that way. So if you want safety, security, and joy, while your partner wants aliveness, daring, and passion, you as a couple have some fun ahead; now you get to take each other to these new places

You may also start to find you have a lot more in common and a lot of things you like to do together. You can develop a new pattern or way of being as a couple. And life together can be a constantly growing experience of learning to give and to receive in fresh ways. When your relationship is this strong, when it overflows with this ch love, then it spills into all parts of your life and work, your family's experience, and how your friends feel around you. Everything gets the overflow of emotion, and you get to have the extra energy to enjoy more and to give more.

Now ...

After you have both completed your lists, exchange them. I want you to brainstorm together. Don't worry if you are doing this without your partner, find ways to ask them how they like to feel. When needed take an educated guess by observing their emotions. Make their list for yourself to learn from and to give to them through.

Sometimes, your best ideas will come the next day; you can write them down and share them again. This week pick one thing to do for your partner from this list every day. Remember, the list was made by your partner and your selection will be directly related to the ways in which he or she is able to feel best around you.

For example, let's say one of your desires is to feel appreciated and your partner embraces you passionately after dinner. You may be holding a dirty plate or you may have a toddler pulling at your jeans. It doesn't matter; there are no excuses for not accepting this hug. Listen to your partner and appreciate how he or she just appreciated you. Reward your partner with your love and your energy — a smile, a word, a gesture. This is how you are going to be able to access all those delicious feelings. If the timing is truly bad — the dog is dragging the turkey off the table right as your wife is nibbling at your ear — then ask for a redo. You can just rewind and say, "I need to really take in how you were just loving me." Then later ask for a chance to revisit the moment or take action to recreate it. This time be present ... and enjoy the attention and connection.

CHAPTER 3

Love Strengths

Now that we've begun the process of getting to know ourselves and our own emotional needs, as well as beginning to look honestly at our partner's emotional needs, let's talk about your specific love strengths.

Following is a series of stem statements. Please take some time to complete each one. Let yourself be honest and free when responding. Once you have completed this brief activity, we're going to figure out ways for you to use what you already have.

FIVE STEM STATEMENTS:

(Write down as many answers as come to you.)

It is easy for me to show my love by...

I can ...
to make him/her feel my love.

I can ...
to get him/her in the mood for making love.

When I ...
it makes him/her smile or laugh.

When I ...
I get us excited about our love.

Congratulations, you have just created your cheat sheet! This list will help you figure out what you can do when you've forgotten what to do.

I'd like you to put the answers to these questions in some strategic places. This means literally placing it somewhere. How about in the freezer where you keep the ice-cream so that next time you reach out to connect with Ben and Jerry or with the Hagen Das family, you immediately remember how to also connect with your partner? Perhaps you should put the list in the drawer where you keep the remote control, or stick it on your computer, phone, or iPad, or under your pillow or on your bathroom mirror.

These are your strengths, so there's no reason not to use them every day. Make it easy to be happy by doing what works for you — and for your lover. Your list will grow and you should check in with yourself on the first day of every month, setting a 10-minute appointment in your calendar for you to revisit your strengths.

Ask yourself these questions again. Add to your list. See what works for you. If something has stopped working, then just take it off the list. Let another strength replace it. There's no need to stay with something that isn't working, and you make room for what does!

CHAPTER 4

The Fantastic Five

What is a proven way to make a relationship better? I'm going to share the secret to every successful marriage or relationship — the Fantastic Five. These five simple and fantastic practices — the secrets of loving couples — are meant for you to do every day, no matter what.

When we ask successful couples what they do every day to show trust, love, and kindness to each other, they reveal the following practices. Each practice takes only seconds, but it will create ripples of good feeling that will impact every part of your relationship. If you have children, they'll learn by watching you, and in the future they will know how to be happy in a relationship too.

THE FANTASTIC FIVE:

1. SPECIAL COMPLIMENTS.

Compliment your partner's physical appearance. Every day you should tell your wife or husband, "You are so beautiful (or handsome)." Notice details. And make sure to compliment your partner every day in some way, even if the compliment goes unnoticed. The compliments don't need to be original: "Your eyes are beautiful," "I love your shoulders," "Your smile is the best way to start the day." Just give the compliment and appreciate the person physically.

The more you do this, the more you'll see details that you appreciate. You will be filling your partner up with positive thoughts too: "My partner is attracted to me and appreciates me."

It's also really important to compliment your partner's spirit: "You feel so much." "I admire your dedication to work." "I admire your way with the kids." However, these compliments don't replace the physical compliments — they are the frosting on the cake.

Now, how often should you compliment your partner? All the time. I know some people are implicit communicators — they think, rather than say. They think, "Hey, I already said this earlier, no need to repeat it. She knows. He knows." Not true. If you're the kind of person who doesn't like to repeat what you've said, then you're going to have to change. Complimenting your partner regularly, even when it feels repetitive, is important. If you're a person of few words, then you need to develop two or three ways to explicitly show what you mean. This effort you make will come back to you many times in the loving gestures your partner gives you.

2. Politeness.

Be polite (unless you're playing in the bedroom).

Successful couples are polite to each other. They ask for favors respectfully and they show gratitude. Most important, they never take the other for granted. So, when your partner offers to get something for you, you appreciate it and respond with a thoughtful sentence: "Thank you for taking care of me." We all want to be respected, valued, and treated as an equal with consideration. So show it. People are not mind-readers and what we learned in preschool counts right now. It doesn't matter if you are spirited and like to argue, or tend to be quiet and introspective, you still need to show respect and gratitude.

3. The Kiss.

Every day, there needs to be one romantic kiss. Stop and focus for 30 seconds entirely on your partner. Focus on the kiss. Ask for guidance: "Do you like it when...?" Try different styles. Choose a time for this kiss so you won't forget. Tell the other person, "I'm going to kiss you now, so you can't think about anything else for this minute." If she's been rejecting you for years, then it's certainly time to kiss her. If he's been a workaholic or a cheater or just an asshole, but you want this relationship to work, then kiss him today and every day. There is no excuse for not sharing one kiss a day. Even if for some reason you hate mouth-to-mouth contact, you still need to kiss. You can use your fingers to caress your partner's lips, kiss your partner's hair, or press your lips anywhere you enjoying kissing. I respect all styles, but ask you to find a way to give to your partner at this level of intimacy no matter your style. Be creative.

There are likely many couples who are reading this book who have stopped all physical contact. It's not too late though. You must suspect this if you are still with me. If the idea of kissing your partner is overwhelming, you can start by just touching a neutral part of his or her body. You may want to pat him on the back or ask if you can give her a hug or shoulder rub. As you take this step to reach out physically it will become easier to start kissing. Spend a little time remembering what it was like to be lovers. Instead of invoking shame or guilt over loss of connection, tell your partner that moving forward you are going to initiate touch and kissing. Most of us crave this physical attention.

If your partner says no to you — which is rare by the way — then it is time to ask what happened that made the person afraid to open to you at the physical level. Was there a time that a big breach of trust took place? Let your partner know you are ready to take responsibility for that past action. Keep reading and you will find patterns for rebuilding this trust and then bringing the intimacy back into your relationship.

4. THE GREETING.

Change the way you greet your partner when you reunite in the evening after work. Surprise him or her. Think for a second right now about how your greeting could be different: more exciting, more loving, happier. What I love about the greeting is that it's only about a minute long, yet it can change the tone of the whole evening.

Get creative — put on some music. Arrange to meet in a different location. Be funny and surprising. Grab his butt. Or get on your knees and tell her she's gorgeous. Every greeting after being apart is a chance to make the relationship new. So go for it. I know most days won't be works of art, but a hug or a sweet whisper can have great effect. Smile super warmly, present a flower, and offer your full attention. If you are very organized, then throw it all together with a compliment, a kiss, and an amazing greeting. Follow it with #5 — a commitment of your love.

5. DAILY COMMITMENT.
Happy couples tell each other every day that they are committed and that they love each other. It only takes one person to start this practice. Maybe things have been rocky for a while or the day was really rough. It's okay. What is essential is that you remember the deeper truth: that you love this person, you choose this person, and you choose to be committed to this person. When you take the time to tell your partner, you are also reminding yourself of what really matters to you, what is underneath and what is important. You are shifting the focus to the priority of your love.

And even if you have been mad for a long time and you think your partner needs to change, remember that it all starts with your love. You have this incredible power to get your partner to really see and experience your steadfast support. And it's really simple: "I love you. I'm committed to you. I'm here for you. This is our life. I want you to know how much you matter." Put this in your own words and just do it; commit with words to the higher purpose and expression of your relationship. When you need extra power for this gesture, return to your power place — remember that place where you feel peaceful and whole, a particular room, the garden, on the beach — and let yourself be there for a minute, and then speak your words of commitment.

Now, let's brainstorm together by going through this list again. I'd like you to visualize each daily practice, and then write down your ideas for it.

1. SPECIAL COMPLIMENTS:
Ideas
Times
Details

2. POLITENESS:
How do I show that I appreciate what he or she does?
How and when can I do this more?

3. THE KISS:
What kind of kiss does he or she like?
How long should I make the kiss?
What can I add in to really please my partner?

4. THE GREETING:
Some surprising details I will add.
What would he or she like me to express?
What words will I use?
What do I need to think about right before sharing the greeting in order to show up with energetic presence?

5. DAILY COMMITMENT:
Today, how can I commit with words and presence?
How does my commitment today reflect our future love?
How will this commitment make my partner happy?
How will this commitment help me be confident and more present?

Here's a Bonus:
Are you ready to turn up the heat in your relationship?

Then find a way to tell your partner that you want him or her physically. This could be conveyed through a look, with spoken words, in a text, or in an email. What counts is that you are communicating your desire. Follow up with actions. Now, if your partner isn't ready and your communication is rejected, remember you are showing your passion and it is being noticed. Your partner will warm up eventually. Everyone takes his or her own time, but I promise, your efforts will be appreciated because your partner is most certainly starting to get how much appreciation, love, commitment, and desire you have.

CHAPTER 5

Destructive Patterns

It is time to stop a negative pattern you're caught in, move away from the relationship trap you keep falling into. We all have one.

MEET GENINE AND TOM

I'm going to tell you the story of a client named Genine, who faced, and eventually escaped, a deeply negative pattern. Genine found herself constantly calling her husband at work to check on him. She wanted to see if he was okay and to get him to connect with her and talk to her about his day.

Tom, her husband, always complained about anxiety. And Genine knew that when the anxiety became too much, he would either overeat to sooth himself or he'd masturbate with pornography. Over their five-year marriage, Genine had convinced herself it was her job to babysit Tom's emotions so this wouldn't happen. She had also convinced herself that if Tom overate or masturbated, it was a reflection of her failure as a lover and proof that he didn't fully love her.

From Tom's point of view, the "babysitting" behavior of checking on him was evidence that Genine didn't trust him. He felt a lack of freedom and independence. He assured Genine that neither of his negative behaviors had anything to do with her. Of course, this didn't soothe Genine in the least. She craved reassurance that Tom had, as she put it, "Only eyes for her." If he watched pornography and then masturbated, or even turned to rich foods, she felt this meant he didn't truly love her.

First, I needed to help Genine with her pattern of incessantly checking on her husband. Instead of asking her to use her willpower or to re-pattern her behavior or meet her needs for connection and certainty by herself, I told her that the behavior was a great thing. Her calling, e-mailing, and texting her husband during the day was proof of how much she loves him. I asked her to agree to communicate with him at least four times per day. Up to then, she said it was usually three times a day. The rule now was she had to communicate with him in a loving way. She was to let him know she appreciated and admired him, and that she was excited about seeing him in the evening. Tom was only required to say, "Great," "Wonderful," or "Can't wait." I also asked him to reassure Genine before he left for work that he loved her and only had eyes for her.

This new pattern worked for the couple because Genine was expressing the truth that lay beneath her nagging and needy behavior. She wasn't playing a game to get attention; instead, she was directly giving love to Tom. In this way, she connected with him authentically. She showed him — and herself — her true loving nature and higher purpose. I suggested that Genine ask Tom to set a reminder on his phone for the other daily things she had nagged him about, like drinking water or eating fruit. She also agreed to cook tasty healthy foods for him in the evening and not give him a hard time if he wanted to take her out to dinner. She could help him break the habit of overeating rich foods, which had led to some serious health problems, without rejecting his overtures of love, such as taking her out to dinner.

So how does this apply to you? Like Genine, perhaps you have a pattern — most people do — of asking for something that gives you a sense of connection but also creates friction in the relationship. Think for a moment. Scan your communications. If a pattern similar to Genine's pops out at you, then ask yourself what emotion is underneath the surface. What do you want to let your partner know on the deepest level? Consider how you might replace that habitual request with expressions of your true nature, your deep commitment, love, or excitement. Go to that power place and ask the question, "What really lies beneath this pattern?"

The answer may come to you instantly. Or, it maybe a question to sit with for a few days. Patterns are tricky and they give to us in some way. Keep in mind that even when a pattern is hurtful, we keep returning to it because the hurt is familiar and safe. I always remind people that our problem patterns serve a purpose. If, rather than ignoring a pattern or blaming our partner for it, we become friends with it, the pattern will reveal its deeper purpose to us.

Emotional Bank Deposits

As we have said, one way in the world can be misunderstood when it crosses another way! Let's say you are a true free spirit who values space and personal freedom. This can easily be received in a negative way by a partner. Here's an idea: I'd like you to come up with three ways to tell your partner every day how much you adore him or her. Get detailed. The more specific you can be what you love about your partner, the more he or she will feel it. You are investing in your emotional bank account with your partner!

And when your partner has moments of low self-esteem or when you are less than loving, these expressions will help balance out the moments of being out of sync. Your partner will feel, know, and experience your love daily, not just when he or she does something for you or achieves something in the world. In this way, your partner gets to experience your love "just because."

These expressions fill up the relationship bank account — and it takes about three deposits for every withdrawal to create a healthy love account.

Let's explore this image a little further. Every relationship can be viewed as a container for experiences, communications, and feelings. When our container or bank account is full of good "deposits," the times in which we screw up or make a withdrawal can be offset. It's normal to feel off kilter or say something hurtful from time to time, and it only turns into a problem when there is not enough good feeling to counter the rough patch. By regularly contributing "love bank deposits," the container will fill up and the relationship will be more protected.

CHAPTER 6

Love Modality

What if my partner doesn't believe I love him or her? In addition to the ways we express love, and our love styles, we have modes of reception for love. These modalities may be familiar because they are also the ways that we learn: visual, auditory, and kinesthetic.

How best can your partner receive your love? Sometimes partners who deeply love one another get stuck because they have a simple difference in their ways of receiving.

One person, for example, is kinesthetic, so she experiences the world through touch and feeling, while her husband is auditory, so he understands and connects on a deep level to what he hears. So what happens when these two people attempt to communicate? She keeps touching him to show her love and waiting for him to touch her in the right way. Meanwhile, he never really gets it even though he tries. His touch is a bit rough or maybe it's too gentle. She doesn't feel his presence.

At the same time, he keeps telling her he loves her because it's what he wants to hear. She barely hears him and thus doesn't know to reciprocate in the way he is hoping for because she is focused on the fact he hasn't touched her in the right way. So, these two people know intellectually that they love each other, but they don't feel it.

Some of us know our preferred modality: auditory, visual, or kinesthetic. Don't freak out if you're thinking, "I have no idea what I am or what my partner is." Or maybe you're realizing, "Wow, maybe I've been getting it all wrong." This lesson is about figuring it out, figuring yourself out, and figuring your partner out. So I'm going to ask you some questions. If you are in a relationship, feel free to ask your partner these questions later.

HOW DO YOU LIKE TO LEARN? Reading would be considered visual, doing and experiencing would be kinesthetic, and listening to audio or live teaching would be auditory.

WHAT TURNS YOU ON MOST? A whispered loving compliment? This would be auditory. To see your lover looking gorgeous and happy? Obviously, this is visual. (And in our highly visual culture, we are all visual to some degree.) But if you like to see movies, instead of reading, or if you paint or take photographs or videos, then you're probably extra visual. Or, maybe your best memories with your partner are of something like hiking together, taking a class, playing a game, exercising or cooking together Then you must be kinesthetic.

Once you understand which modality works best for you and your lover, I want you to experience all three this week. Do something visual for your partner, such as taking a photo. Do something auditory, such as playing music or saying something meaningful. Then do something kinesthetic, such as giving a massage or playing a game, like Twister or Wii.

Then I suggest that you give to your partner every day in this specific way. If the person is visual, then look into his or her eyes more often. Keep in mind that even if you are auditory and would rather listen to your partner's voice, your partner needs to be seen by you. Your partner needs you to say that you see him or her. Your partner may also like you to talk in visual metaphors, such as "I see us taking a great trip together" or "I can imagine you on the beach or in your snow suit on a mountain." Visual people love imagistic talk. They experience the world in pictures. So, when you speak about your joy and connection through images, it is received in a special way.

If your partner is auditory, then remember that hearing you is most important. Pay attention to your tone of voice. Flood your partner with sweet, loving words. Say sexy naughty things to your partner. Give your partner a nickname. Nicknames are another sign of love, connection, trust, and playfulness. A nickname usually indicates a special confidence in the area of relationships.

If your partner is kinesthetic, then he or she loves to be touched and be active in a physical sense. You might give this type of partner a massage every day. Before saying anything, touching your partner will enhance connection. Hugging, kissing, and stroking ... playing with your partner's hair ... holding hands. You can have fun exploring. And your partner will hear you at a whole new level because you have just opened up the channels for taking you in and feeling your love. This step leads to greater mutual understanding.

It is human nature to want to reciprocate. And when we are understood and communicated with in the vocabularies that are most natural for us, our instinct is to give back fully.

If I were stranded on a couples retreat with only one skill to teach, it just might be to understand your partner's modality. I suggest taking it seriously and being playful both. Don't wait. Connect through the modalities that are most conducive to actually connecting!

(By the way, if you are in a long-distance relationship, don't worry, you can invoke visually, share mood through music, and talk touch!)

Now let's get some ideas down in writing.
Modalities:

My preferred modality is ...
I will tell my partner about my modality in a loving way by ...

My partner's preferred modality is …

I will give to my partner through his or her modality in this way …

CHAPTER 7

Creating Greater Connection

It's fair to say that every person in a relationship wants to experience connection. Take a quick moment right now, before I put any ideas or words in your head, to write down what connection means to you.

How does it feel to be connected to your husband, wife, girlfriend, or boyfriend? By connection, I mean a unique experience of feeling linked together with only your partner. Write down how it feels to be connected to your partner and no one else.

GIVE YOURSELF THREE MINUTES TO WRITE.

Connection means …
Connection means …
Connection means …

Okay, let's get real. The reason for focusing on the feeling and experience of connection is that most of us have a romantic view of connection that is based in books, movies, and songs. Or we have a jaded view that has evolved by witnessing the poor relationships of our parents, our friends, the couples around us, or our own previous relationships.

What is wrong with these two views of connection, the romantic and the jaded? Chances are, if you are feeling like you want more from your relationship, then you want more connection. And because we all have such a variety of life experiences and expectations of connection, we inevitably are disappointed when a partner doesn't connect in the way we expect. And then many of us go back and forth on how to get what we want. Simply saying what we want feels unromantic. But dropping subtle hints may appear to be ineffective.

Meet Sally and Nick

I'm going to tell you the story of a really great couple, Sally and Nick. If you saw them at the gym or in the park, you would think they were very well matched. They met as children, and then got back together after college and are now around 40 years old. They got married and had a son. Unfortunately, neither was very happy with the relationship. They said they wanted nothing more than to be happy together. However, their expectations were as different as different could be.

I learned this right away when I asked Sally to write to me about her ideal day. I didn't even ask for the story to include her husband. Sally wrote a lovely letter outlining a day of being with her husband, having a picnic together outside, sitting by a cozy fire, and reading next to each other. She described a beautiful dinner served by another person, just for them, in the privacy of their own living room.

I was frankly surprised by what Sally had written. When I ask a woman of this age with a child to describe her ideal day, it usually entails a lot of time for herself, doing exciting or relaxing things, being away from the home, having an escape day or vacation day. Sally's description told me how strongly she craves deep connection in the form of physical presence, being observers of the world together, and enjoying small pleasant daily experiences with her man. Her living room or yard sufficed as the ideal environment. However, she needed her husband by her side with his attention on her.

Now let me tell you about her husband Nick. Nick is all about doing, achieving, following a plan, and doing the right thing. He has dealt with his sexless marriage by working out at least two hours every day. He wants Sally to be happy, but he struggles with really listening to what she says. For him a great day is full of outdoor accomplishments, getting to a certain point on the river, playing a high caliber golf game, or learning to fly a plane.

But Sally and Nick love each other, and they've loved each other their whole lives. Why aren't they happy as a couple? They want to be happy. They want to have passion again. They want to enjoy weekends together. Yet the to-do list is always more important to Nick than the moment of being together, and he can't understand why they should go on dates. Activities such as romantic dinners and picnics strike him as wasteful and non-productive, whereas Sally sees them as opportunities for deep connection.

While talking to Sally and Nick in a session, I learned that early in their courtship and marriage Nick would make up stories for Sally that he'd share in bed late at night. Now, Sally is flooded by pain late at night about the emotional state of the marriage and so she complains to Nick. He is very tired and cannot see any way to make it better. He feels she focuses on the negative all the time and that she compares their marriage to other marriages, many of which are fictional.

So what's going wrong here? Can two such different people ever feel really connected? Let's start with what is wrong. First, they haven't really explored what the other enjoys. And, in the moments when they do get it, the response is to think, feel, and perhaps really believe that what the other wants is in some way wrong. In this pattern, the solution to the marriage problem is to fix the partner!

The truth is that the real answer is that both partners must pause and learn something new: to appreciate what the other wants.

This means that Nick must get to the feeling that what Sally wants is great. She wants just to be together. She wants to be able to analyze, talk, and hold hands, without needing to get anything done. She wants to dance with Nick, go out to dinner, sit and look up at the clouds on a beautiful day.

Until now, Nick has wanted adventure and to achieve various goals — and he has also wanted a sexual connection with Sally. And he has never before put it together that Sally cannot really trust him with intimacy because it is things like an afternoon around the house being lazy together that establish feelings of safety for her.

And Sally? When Sally understood how terrible it felt for Nick to be rejected sexually she was able to shift radically overnight and show him physical love again. All I asked her to do was make one offer of love to him. This could have been a kiss or hug. She chose to take off her clothes and sit on his lap. She later asked me, "Does that count as an offer?"

When Nick understood the importance of dinner dates and other romantic experiences, he also went all the way. Sally reported delightedly that he had started going to Zumba classes with her. It is often the case that a couple has a lot of good in the relationship to be mined but when sexual intimacy becomes blocked, the couple panics. This is when it is especially important to remember all that you have — and imagine all that you can now create together.

Sally and Nick found new passion, trust, and joy together again by taking some risks. They needed a coach to help translate their love modalities and to point out that it wasn't their desires that were causing problems but their communications. Not only were the desires reasonable, they were healthy!

For many couples, understanding and connecting in the way that works for each partner results in deeper trust, intimacy, and sexual pleasure. Stretching yourself emotionally, being fearless, and giving to your man or woman in a way that he or she can receive will result in more trust and intimacy. When both partners feel understood and emotionally connected, sexual intimacy will feel more natural, more organic, more energized, and ... well ... more intimate!

For a woman, great sex often means being able to let go. Being really open and risky in bed can be scary, so what helps is for her to feel understood and to know she can trust her partner. Sex isn't a trade-off; it is an extension of the connection your relationship already has.

So, let's go back to the steps you can take. Start by writing down your dream day with your partner. How would you include him or her? How do you like to connect? Be real and honest. If you like to shop together, write that down. If you like to talk about work, write that down. If you like to drink and forget about the world, write that down. There is no "correct" dream day, only your dream way. Also, think about this day in your current life, not a day from the past or in the future.

HERE IS YOUR HEADING: MY DREAM DAY ...
(fill in what follows)

What happens when you connect in the way that works for both of you? It multiplies. You start to find more and more things you can do together that extend this feeling of connection.

After writing down your dream day, sit with your partner and describe it. Explain the vibe you like to share or the level of conversation you like.

Next, commit to spending one-to-two hours together each week that involves an aspect of your dream day. All you need is two hours together where you're connecting the way your partner wants to connect. Work within the parameters of your life so that it can be incorporated. This commitment is to a total of four hours each week, which don't include time devoted to sexual intimacy. This time is focused on other forms of connecting. If you have kids or need to be apart one week, work around it. You know you can do it if you are serious about it. Two hours per week for each of you. Be flexible and creative. For example, if what she really wants is a foot rub that takes 10 minutes, let her know you want to do that for her every night.

This level of sharing dream days and activities offers a very deep form of connection. It reflects a wonderful step toward forging a thriving relationship.

Now, if you share with your partner and receive a startled look or no response at all, don't panic! Sometimes a partner may be surprised, or feel guilty, or interpret the dream days as threatening. Ask yourself if you could share in a less threatening way or in a more inclusive way. An opening such as, "At some point, I'd love to ... with you," might be easier for your partner than, "If you and I would only ...." Even something like, "I've never told you before but I have a dream fantasy of..." can be hard to hear. This is often the tone that comes out when a person has repressed many personal desires and needs for a long time. When this person finally shares, it can sound like hurt and anger. Remember, being clear about why you are sharing is critical. You share your dream days with your partner so he or she understands you not to point out what hasn't occurred before. This approach will expand your connection, trust, and intimacy. Through exploring your dream day internally you are also growing in your own ability to feel passionate, know what you like, and take leadership and control of your powerful love.

CHAPTER 8

Our Many Marriages

Here's a question for you: "How many marriages do you really have?"

What we as coaches have found over and over again is that no one has just one marriage. If you are thinking, "Sure, there are polygamists out there; I've watched Big Love," this isn't what we mean. This idea developed in a coaching session we had with a woman named Linda. Linda was talking with me about how disappointed she was with her husband. Even though they had been married for 25 years, Rick just didn't seem to have his wife's back. When Linda got sick, it was her mother or sisters who came to her aid. Her husband actually seemed to blame her and think her sicknesses were psychosomatic. Oddly, years earlier, she had started to have symptoms like anxiety attacks, and he was supportive and soothing. Now that she was physically ill, which also caused anxiety, he responded only with frustration.

Linda was a deeply committed person and she loved Rick, but this behavior really worried her. She worried about what would happen if she suffered a life-threatening illness. "Is he really there for me?" she wondered.

Rick and Linda had six children and also had big parenting issues. They had opposite views on boundaries when it came to their adolescents. Linda tended to give in to Rick's rules or, more accurately, his lack of rules, so as not to create further stress in their relationship. But this ended up making her even more anxious because she worried about the safety of their kids. Rick didn't believe in curfews and he felt that drinking was simply a part of life. He said in front of the kids that it was normal to drink and drive sometimes. Even though their son was arrested for a DUI, Rick refused to change his tune.

As coaches, we felt pretty torn here. This couple had a lot wrong. Our client, Linda, felt deep commitment in spite of the pain. The question was how to support and elevate Linda, and help to improve the marriage, when Rick refused to even speak with us. Well, Plato said it well: Necessity is the mother of invention. The question to shape: How many marriages do you really have?

I explained to Linda that in every single marriage there are actually many marriages. The details are context-specific — You may have a marriage as parents, as runners, as extended family, as friends. There is, perhaps, your spiritual marriage, your social marriage, your professional. All couples have many different marriages inside of their one marriage.

I asked Linda to tell me Rick's greatest strengths. As we spoke, it became clear that Rick was a fun husband. He showed Linda a good time. No one could show her as good a time as he could, whether they were at Disneyland (without the kids) or at home. Their talks and their outings were completely enjoyable, as long as they weren't focused on the kids, household rules, finances, or on Linda's sicknesses. And Linda reported that their sex was pretty good too. So, I made a proposal, "Let's find the best marriage out of your many marriages." Linda quickly answered that their social marriage was the best.

The only complaint Linda had in this marriage was that she wished Rick would care more about his fitness. Linda shared that the only complaint Rick had was that Linda needed to show him that she wanted to have sex more often. This told us that their marriage as lovers was very strong too and just needed to be tweaked by a few honest communications. There were things Linda could do without even discussing them with Rick that would take their very strong passion to over-the-top passion. When Linda figured out the ingredients for the "Lovers Marriage" and then mixed them with the great experiences of being more active together and letting herself find her goddess more often in the bedroom, she was able to create two amazing marriages. The "Social Marriage" and the "Lovers Marriage" merged.

This shift meant that the question was no longer how to help a "broken" marriage. The question was, how do we help a marriage that already has two amazing marriages within it? The two marriages that needed help were the "Marriage as Parents" and "Marriage as Illness Support."

Linda had an impressive support system of family and friends who went with her to doctors' appointments and talked her through anxiety attacks in the middle of the night. Her relatives and friends provided a lot of support because she was a truly giving and loving person. I asked her if it would be okay to just let her husband off the hook on the illness support role, since she really did have that covered. And since Rick was so much fun, I reminded her that she wouldn't want that to change. Wasn't it better to just let the Social Marriage and the Lovers Marriage be the most important? She agreed. And she even realized that if he was worrying about her, he wouldn't be able to show her such a good time. With this clarified, she also began to experience his humor and good social attitude as a powerful healing source for her body.

Now, we had only one tough marriage on our hands — and three happy marriages. The remaining challenge was the Marriage as Parents. Fortunately, after experiencing a more loving and exciting time with Linda, Rick agreed to start being a part of the coaching. When we spoke to the couple together, Rick's loving nature as a father became very clear, and we learned that his rules came from a philosophical stance. The work we needed to do as coaches now entailed really understanding each of their rules when it came to the children and helping them to find areas of agreement. The resolution wasn't going to be in one person's court. We would encourage the couple to really hear each other in order to enable positive compromise. When there is a feeling of excitement about one or two of your marriages, a challenging marriage can be navigated from a much more balanced position.

Rick and Linda kept focusing on their strong marriages. From this place of strength, they were able to create new rules that honored the playful part of Rick and the concerned part of Linda. The parents' alignment meant that the kids had less to rebel against. Often a teenager acts out to draw attention to the child's bad behavior, thereby uniting the parents through a common focus. Without knowing it, they are hurting themselves to save the parents' marriage. Eventually, of course, this strategy stops working. A child of any age feels great relief when the parents present a united front.

How many marriages are inside your marriage?

I'd like you to take two minutes now to consider the question now that you understand what we mean. Write down all the marriages you have. It can be helpful to do this exercise even if you are not married but are in a committed relationship or have been in the past.

Give a name to each of the marriages. Here are some examples:

Friends Marriage
Co-Workers Marriage
Extended Family Marriage
Social Marriage
Runners/Kayakers/Opera Marriage
Explorers Marriage
Lovers Marriage
Social Activists Marriage
Pet Owners Marriage

Now, just insert the name of each marriage below. You will go back to the "More" and "Never" sections later. By the way, you may or may not have as many marriages as we leave space for — and a few of you may even have additional!

Our many marriages:

1. Name of marriage:
More 1:
More 2:
Never 1:
Never 2:

2. Name of marriage:
More 1:
More 2:
Never 1:
Never 2:

3. Name of marriage:
More 1:
More 2:
Never 1:
Never 2:

4. Name of marriage:
More 1:
More 2:
Never 1:
Never 2:

5. Name of marriage:
More 1:
More 2:
Never 1:
Never 2:

6. Name of marriage:
More 1:
More 2:
Never 1:
Never 2:

7. Name of marriage:
More 1:
More 2:
Never 1:
Never 2:

Okay, let's go to the next step and find out what is really strong in each of your marriages.

Under your marriage headings, note some additional details. You are creating a more list for each marriage, meaning, "I want more of ...". Make two entries for each marriage.

Next, work on your list of what should never happen in each marriage. Under each heading, you are going to offer two things that never should happen. It is useful to let a partner know your limits. When we are honest about our limits, a partner has a really good chance at succeeding in meeting our needs.

Let me offer an illustration. Let's take a Social Marriage as our example. This couple goes out and experiences their social time together as a significant part of their relationship. They might vacation with friends, have dinner with friends, and friends might drop by all the time, etc.

The wife's "more" entries might be:
I want to have dinner parties at our house once a week.
I want to have new friends with healthier lifestyles.

Her "never" entries might be:
We should never flirt with each other's friends.
You should invite me every time you make plans with friends; never assume that I know I am invited.

These are actionable parameters. This is not about needs or emotions. This is more like a game plan, a map for the different marriages. Of course, the entries will change, and it's a great idea to do this exercise every few months or whenever you need to update the marriage.

If you haven't done it yet, take time now to fill in the missing information. It is missing for both of you!

CHAPTER 9

Rules & Jealousy

Have you been testing your partner? What happens when one person's rules are different from another's? Imagine that building a relationship is like building a house. Let's say you have the same rules, the same values, the same practices, the same friends, the same strengths, the same parenting ideas, the same diet, the same exercise interests, and the same communication skills. So, when you are building your house, everything is perfectly symmetrical. All of your beams line up just right, and your walls are straight. Unfortunately, every room looks the same. Your living room is no different than the dining room. There is no variation in the textures or depths of color. But guess what? There are no surprises. The house looks just like you'd expect it to look: predictable and a little boring. Without the interesting angles, nooks, and curves which make architecture beautiful.

If relationships were houses, they wouldn't be perfectly symmetrical structures, right? Why is that? Because people aren't straightforward in this way. And we aren't the same as each other. Two tiles may be but two people are not. We haven't had the same life experiences, and we don't share exactly the same dreams, even when we think we do. And our personalities and preferences are unique to us.

We have some pretty crazy rules — and beliefs too. These rules and beliefs are our own. Many of them are not even revealed until a new situation comes up. Imagine a woman home with the children, exhausted, struggling with her self-image and sense of meaning. Now, imagine her husband works in an office that is filled with smart, confident women. This never-before-jealous woman (the wife) may find herself overwhelmed with anger every time her husband so much as mentions a female co-worker. The other side of the coin? Suddenly, out of nowhere, the man feels his wife doesn't trust him. She doesn't seem to appreciate or even notice how hard he works for their family. And he has no idea how to get her to feel loved by him again.

In another illustration, a man may have expected his wife to work outside the home. When they were dating and early in their marriage, she had spoken about how important it was for a mother to stay home with kids, but she spoke in generalizations, never saying directly that after having a child she'd rather struggle financially than work. He took it for granted that they would both work.

So, this husband starts to hint that it is time for his wife to contribute to the family income. He asks her questions about returning to work. When she resists his hints, the tension grows.

Fast forward two years. She's home with their daughter, and his contracting business is in a slump. At this point, he no longer hints, he presses her to go back to teaching. In response, this woman may experience his behavior as a rejection of her deepest core value.

The original misinterpretations have begun to become more and more entangled, mixing with the vicissitudes of life. Now an otherwise happy couple doesn't quite trust each other.

With these confusions, miscommunications, and misunderstandings swirling, this couple isn't going to be in a good place in another two years. If they don't shift gears, learning to hear each other's deeper concerns and not simply going on their own assumptions, they will most likely end up divorced.

There is a myth that happy people, including couples, never feel negative emotions. We know intellectually that it's a misconception but internally we kind of don't. The truth is that successful couples get jealous and experience other negative feelings, but instead of becoming terrified and frozen by a "negative" emotion, the individuals feel secure enough in themselves and in their love for each other to try to understand what is really happening between them. Feelings such as jealousy are a real part of the person's experience, whatever they are based on. We need to seek to better understand more about how the other feels rather than running for the hills. Emotionally speaking, the hills are far away from the scary emotions.

Jealousy: The Big One

Jealousy is a particularly destructive emotion if left unchecked. It can be triggered by the in-laws, work, the iPhone or iPad, friends, the gym, the company, running marathons, yoga class, business trips, a sibling, the kids, Facebook, a past boyfriend or girlfriend, a hobby or advocation — the list is endless. As humans we can be jealous about almost anything. As a loving, successful, and happy couple, we need to understand this rather than react to it by telling the partner that he or she is nuts and just has to get over it. Jealousy is an emotion triggered by a person, thing, place, activity, or a memory. Even when jealousy is triggered by an imagined interaction, it seems very real to the person experiencing it. What we can do is understand the jealousy, its triggers, and what soothes it. Then we can fill our partner with enough love and commitment to convince the person that it is safe to ask for reassurance when it is needed.

Jealousy is like a snowball. When the snowball is small, you can gently release its particles into the air. If you keep rolling it around on the ground, however, it will become a big icy boulder that is hard to budge. The only way it will melt is if it sits in the sun. If your wife or husband is jealous, then you can be the hand that takes up the small snowball and lets it become flakes in the air. If things have been avoided for some time and you are faced with a boulder, you will need to become the sun. If you experience yourself as the ice boulder, you too can create a relationship that like the sun will gently melt the ice.

No matter the situation, I think you owe it to yourself and to your partner to try to understand the jealousy from his or her perspective and to explain it from yours. Let your partner be your warm, direct, and powerful sunlight. Let your partner melt through your layers of ice. Or become that for your partner. This way, any future jealousy can be carried away on the breeze because you understand what is necessary for the relationship to feel secure.

Here are some questions that will help the person who is jealous overcome those feelings. Sit back and let yourself answer the questions in a relaxed way, no self-judgment and nothing to prove.

First, let's figure out exactly what makes you jealous.

- When does it happen?
- What do you suspect is the need you have underneath your jealousy?
- What could your partner do to help you?

(Write down how you can communicate the actions or words you'd like to experience or hear in a way that honors both your partner's love for you and what is important to him or her.)

Becoming Resourceful

Meet Carey. There are moments when we spin out of control either in our thoughts or feelings. This happens sometimes to a very sweet woman I know named Carey. Carey tends to get stuck in repetitive thoughts every time her husband is late coming home, or when he makes a choice with which she disagrees. She has confided to me that she becomes so upset that it turns to anger and even violence. She will throw a glass or punch a wall. This is very scary for her because she feels that her emotions are out of control.

As we worked together it became clear that the problem lay in a repetitive thought and the feelings attached. I developed a strategy to help Carey, which can be used whenever one wants to gain control and understanding of emotions that are spinning out.

I call this approach "becoming resourceful," and it is very easy. Let's use Carey's thoughts as an example to learn from.

Step one is to understand your thoughts. When Carey is upset, it is hard for her to know exactly why. So the first question is, "What was I thinking before the feeling of anger or sadness overtook me?"

Carey was thinking, "He should not be late."

I then asked Carey if any other thoughts were present or if there was a pattern of other thoughts we could put down on paper. She added, "He is choosing his friends over me." Great, now we had two common repetitive thoughts. Next, we wanted to find out about the underlying emotions.

Step two is to explore what emotions are created through these thoughts. For Carey the feeling of being less important to her husband was the first emotion. The next thought was that he didn't value her needs for timeliness and was late on purpose. I asked her to get even clearer about the emotion that came with this thought. "Anger," she responded. What else I asked? "Sadness and fear," she said, in a softer tone. She was getting into a state of authentic understanding of her thoughts and emotions. This laid the groundwork for becoming more resourceful.

Step three involves expanding your view to include the possibility of the other person's perspective. I asked Carey to come up with three new thoughts about why her husband was late. I was looking for any thoughts that express a fresh perspective or possibility. "Okay," she said, "one could be that his boss made him do something last minute. Another is that traffic was slow. Another is that he is trying to process some hard things from the day before coming home, so he stopped to exercise."

"How do you feel now?" I asked.

"There has been a small shift," she noted. "I can see and feel a little more from his side."

"That is all it takes," I told her. The process is easy.

What we need to remember is to take the time to do the process of getting resourceful. If this is a common pattern for you, I recommend that you set aside a few minutes each day to do this when you are feeling calm.

Think of a common disturbing thought/emotion pattern related to your spouse. Take a moment to figure out the feelings that are connected to your thoughts. Once you have done this, create three new thoughts that reflect the perspective of your partner or the perspective of your highest self, or of life itself, which might be conceived of as a commitment to love, or a strong value such as peace or trust.

You will find that doing this exercise can open the door to you becoming suddenly very resourceful — more connected, compassionate, and understanding. This result will, of course, serve everyone in your life. It is part of developing emotional maturity in which we are aware of our own thoughts and feelings and we are aware of another perspective too. This way we can really embody the strength of being resourceful within — and better understand what might be possible for the other person.

CHAPTER 10

Steps to Prevent Future Jealousy

So prevalent is jealousy among couples that I am compelled to devote specific attention to the prevention of it. No one wants to be jealous. Jealousy develops, however, because people haven't been given a way out of their difficult feelings, and their partners haven't learned how to take control and create certainty. Maybe this rings a bell? If so, the following simple steps will prove very helpful. Trust me, I'm no stranger to the green-eyed goddess!

Two steps to prevent jealousy in yourself and your partner:

1. ASK YOURSELF, "How does my partner feel when jealous?" Get into your partner's head — or your own if you're the jealous one. I want you to have a conversation with your partner in which you pretend to be the other person and he or she pretends to be you. You are going to talk about your trust issues and jealousy for about five minutes. Take the time to describe what you are feeling and why. Then you will ask: "Did I get it right? Do I understand what happens to you when you feel like you can't trust me or you feel jealous? I want to do everything I can to show you my love and to ease your feelings of jealousy."

Keep trying until you understand each other. Remember, if you are A who is married to B, then A will pretend to be B and B will pretend to be A.

2. NEXT, YOU WILL ASK: "What can I do to make you feel better when you get jealous?" Your partner may be hesitant to say what you can do. Sometimes, this happens because your partner is so used to this feeling of jealousy that it has become confused with connection, creativity, and passion. But keep asking and tell your partner, "I want to know the answer because I love you so much. Please tell me what I can do so your jealousy melts away and you can feel my love and connection more directly."

This brief activity provides you with an action plan. If your immediate response is that your partner's question is too hard to process (this is often a reflexive feeling), ask yourself seriously what is more important, your comfort or the love between you and your partner? Imagine the passion that is possible when there is complete trust.

CHAPTER 11

The Disappearing Husband

The following story may sound like fiction, but it is absolutely true. I tell it here because it touches on the essential force of love: love both as a superpower and great gift.

A woman, whom I will call Rebecca, contacted me and sounded incredibly upset. Her husband had disappeared! Our session had been arranged by a concerned coach and good friend. Rebecca had a toddler, lived with relatives, and was pregnant with their second baby. You can imagine her friend's concern when she learned Rebecca's husband was missing, though it wasn't the first time he had disappeared.

As we started talking, Rebecca quickly explained that her husband disappears every year or two for months at a time. Her husband would lose his job as a result, and thus would have to start his life over again upon his return. There were periods when she would have no idea whether or not he was alive. No form of communication worked, neither his phone nor e-mail, but Rebecca loved her husband enough that she simply waited and took him back each time.

This time, however, with a toddler, no money, and a baby on the way, she was at her wit's end. How could she go on in such a relationship? In the past, she had forgiven the absence because when he returned he felt so badly about it. His first wife had left him due to this pattern.

Rebecca had no idea what to do and desperately wanted to do what was best for her, their children, and her husband. But as is often true in extreme life situations, what is "best" was unclear. Rebecca had had to move in with her parents and was not happy living in their house. In the past, the husband had lied extensively to cover up for his disappearances, and now she just didn't know if it would be possible or right to trust him when he returned, assuming he did.

She wondered if she should confront him, or leave him, or make him go to a hospital.

First, I let her know that I had no way of offering an opinion without knowing more about them as individuals and as a couple. So the initial session focused on understanding their relationship and who they were individually. She relaxed a bit and told me he was a very good father, he loved her very much, and he enjoyed activities like cooking, yoga, and excursions into nature. She also told me that he always found new work when he came back and was successful and able to take care of her and their child — until another year passed and he would disappear again.

I asked if what I understood was correct: that if he stopped disappearing, she would be very happy and trusting in their relationship. She said she would, and she sounded relieved. She confessed that she was a difficult person herself, very opinionated and full of fire. She could become quite angry and upset, and she feared this was bad for her pregnancy and for her toddler. I agreed with her that these strong emotions were probably not good when pregnant, and being scared, angry, and fearful were probably things she'd want to work on. So, we agreed that since her husband was not around we could work together on helping her to feel calmer and more peaceful, knowing this would benefit her health, her relationship with her child, and her wellbeing in general.

We arranged to talk again in a few days after setting some goals for daily moments of peace, gratitude, and joy. Even if she did get angry, fiery, or defensive, she would have these moments of good feelings to counter the effects of the negative emotions. It is always important to remember that even in the worst emotional circumstances, a person can still experience moments of peace, gratitude, good intentions, and love. Even if negative emotions come up, this practice of making time for moments of balance helps people get used to feeling the positive emotions they want and need to feel. They are training themselves to feel good.

Two days later, Rebecca e-mailed me that her husband had returned and found her at her parents' house. She needed an emergency session.

When we spoke, I had had a little time to process the situation. I asked her a very important question: "Did your husband have any traumatic experience in his past around the time that he disappears every year?" (Now, I'm not a psychic. I remembered a story from my own childhood about a friend's father who had experienced a severe trauma as a child — he had shot his best friend by accident while they were playing with a gun together. As an adult, he would go somewhere alone on the anniversary of the accident. No one in his family knew what he did but he consistently did this every year for over 20 years.) Rebecca explained that when her husband was a teenager, his mother had committed suicide at the same time of year that he regularly disappeared. I asked her if perhaps this was his very private way of coping with the incredible grief of losing his mother this way. She thought that it was possible he was coping with his continued grief in this way.

I then explained to her that sometimes a person who has gone through incredible loss recreates the loss and tests all the people in his or her life. By disappearing and losing everything and then coming back and rebuilding, her husband was making a very courageous choice. Though very much impacted by her, he was actually acting in a very different way than his mother. She ended her life, ended everything, and never returned to rebuild. Rebecca's husband was actually destroying his world and then recreating it, returning to be the good husband, dedicated worker, and caring father again.

Rebecca was very quiet for a while, and then she said that she had never looked at it that way before. She also shared that one of the things that was so painful about his first wife leaving him because of his behavior was that he had "lost" his children too in that they now lived in a different country.

I asked Rebecca how her husband was doing now that he was back. She said he was very depressed, almost shell-shocked; he seemed unable to talk about much or to do anything. Rebecca was worried that he wouldn't be able to work again this time and that she would be left supporting two babies and living with her family in a terrible situation.

We agreed that since he was a good father and husband, and because she could feel such strong compassion for his pain and the way he processed it as an adult, and she could now see him as courageous for coming back and rebuilding his life each time he destroyed it, she would react differently to his return than she or any other woman had ever done before. We discussed how his mother and his previous wife had both left him. Rebecca could break this pattern by telling her husband she understood his way of coping, and that she thought he was a brave and loving man for returning. She would show him that she was there for him no matter what, and she would not leave him. Rebecca decided this would certainly break his pattern and her own pattern of reacting with intense anger and grief.

We then planned for how she could do three things per day that would help her husband also return to being himself, and to find work again, and get them out of the current living situation with her family. The three actions were fairly simple: to take a walk with him; to encourage him to cook, which was an activity he enjoyed; and to give him a massage or go to a yoga class together. She knew that what would really help would be having sex with him, but she wasn't willing to do that yet. I didn't think this was a problem given that she would be connecting with him in ways he would appreciate — and he would reciprocate in ways that she would appreciate — and slowly their trust and intimacy would return.

To make a long story short, Rebecca's husband was deeply appreciative of her view of his disappearances and of her understanding.

He was grateful that she reached out three times a day to connect with him. In a matter of weeks, they were living on their own again and, what's more, they had decided to start a business together running a bed and breakfast.

The next time we spoke, Rebecca's goal and challenge was to stop being such an intense and, in her own words, aggressive communicator. She needed support to be both a wife and a business partner. Their sex life was back and life had shifted in a very new and dynamic direction.

Through connection and understanding, Rebecca was able to release a destructive pattern in her husband and in herself. She was able to grow and be there in the way that he needed. I have no doubt that her courage to choose to understand and value what was loving and good in her husband paid off for both of them.

Do you have any rituals in your life that help to ease the pain of a past hurt or trauma. If so, write down what they are. Then write down if there is an even better way you could honor the healing process. So, for example, if you eat to soothe a loss, could you instead listen to music you love. If this applies to you. Try creating this new ritual to lessen time spent on the old unconscious ritual. Many of us do small things daily as a coping mechanism for our hurt. We may not disappear for months but we do disappear in small ways daily or weekly. The point of this discovery and new ritual is to fully honor our need to heal from pain by taking action that comes from a loving and truthful part of ourselves.

CHAPTER 12

Forgiving Yourself and Each Other

Chances are if you are human and if you are in a relationship, at some point, maybe even now, you'll need to say you are sorry to someone and you will need to accept an apology. We all do things that are hurtful, and when we don't know how to apologize, or we don't know how to truly accept our partner's apology, it gets us into trouble.

As people we have lots of rules and opinions regarding the best way to express, "I'm sorry." This tendency to judge the quality of an apology according to very personal standards complicates the process for a couple and ends up leaving a lot of gunk in our emotional spaces. Chances are very high that the apology you receive won't be perfect. Surely, if you were to apologize to yourself, you would do a much better job of it. So, let's swallow some bitter medicine right now. This is the emotional medicine that clears the way for health and happiness in your relationship.

Accept the apologies you're given. No matter how imperfect the expression, no matter how much your partner left out, no matter that it wasn't done right ... just accept it. For one minute inhabit the other person's shoes — his or her perspective, painful or nutty past, unique personality, all of it — and then appreciate how much it took for him or her to apologize. You simply need to be with it, take it in, and feel it. This is the nature of acceptance; you heard, you acknowledged, and you decided to move forward. There maybe past apologies that you can remember now. While you remember the past apology apply this new attitude of acceptance.

For many people forgiveness is an emotion that needs permission to be felt. Sometimes we get stuck wanting forgiveness to feel more final. Our desire is for a complete experience of forgiveness as though it could be finalized in an official document — done. Instead, forgiveness is an experience that emerges as intention and emotion. Some people find the emotion of forgiveness easy to create and feel. Others, however, find that it is the intention that allows forgiveness to permeate the atmosphere. You can invoke this by simply speaking to yourself the wish you have to forgive.

In this sense, you didn't necessarily forget, or change your mind, or believe you were wrong to feel hurt — rather, you are valuing love, happiness, and passion over the feelings that keep you from accepting and moving forward. Many couples overcome great suffering through forgiving what was. It only takes one person to forgive past hurts that are blocking the experience of greater love today: YOU.

An idea that really helps me personally is to acknowledge that forgiveness begins with the desire to want to forgive. Even before there is an experience of forgiveness, the desire to be able to forgive starts the process of letting go. You can start with an acknowledgment: I know that the person who hurt me in the past is not the same person today and that when I was hurt he/she was most likely doing what seemed possible given the life and emotional knowledge he/she had at the time.

Often, the one we must forgive is our past self. I can't tell you how many couples suffer from the guilt that one partner carries from a past action that caused the other pain. When this person steps up and forgives his or her past self, room is made for his or her new authentic self to step in.

TAKE A MOMENT, RIGHT NOW, TO ASK YOURSELF:
- Is there something or someone whom I wish to forgive?
- What is a definition of forgiveness I feel good about?
- Do I have any beliefs around forgiveness that limit my being able to experience it? For example, forgiving another will mean I am weak, vulnerable, or uncaring.
- How and when can I begin to simply wish to have this forgiveness daily? Set aside one minute a day for the intention of forgiveness.

CHAPTER 13

Cover Problems

Lots of couples value their cover problem over their desire to be happy and loving together. Many couples that come to coaching tell us their cover problems first. They tell a rather long story that often has the feeling of being rehearsed or regularly repeated.

Meet Jeremy and Susan

A young man named Jeremy started his coaching session by explaining how much he wanted his wife to have greater passion and to want to make love more often. Through our coaching sessions, Susan explained very clearly that greater closeness, trust, and intimacy would lead to more passion. For six weeks the couple worked hard at connecting with each other. They experienced great progress, feelings of love, and amazing sex. Then the lid was blown right off the kettle. What happened?

The in-laws happened. Susan felt less than appreciated by Jeremy's family. And in a state of pain and vulnerability, she said horrible things about them. Later, she apologized — even in writing — with my encouragement.

But a month later, Jeremy still hadn't accepted her apology. He confided to me that he couldn't get the words she had used about his family out of his head. I asked him how his sex life was. He explained that since that night when she exploded, he couldn't find the energy or desire to want his wife sexually. He felt emotionally burned out. I asked if she rejected him, and he said no. A few weeks later his parents visited again. He explained that Susan hadn't spent the day with them this time, and that she had come home for dinner and been polite but not warm.

This is a pretty typical scenario. What Jeremy is doing is saying what he wants with his wife is closeness, intimacy, passion, and sex. His cover story. But it turns out that what he wants more than those things is for his wife to be close with his family and friends. Jeremy is a community lover style but his wife is not.

What Do I Really Want?

So let's think about what you say you want and what you really expect or want. Let's look at expectations. I invite you to honestly express your expectations in writing.

Here's an example:
I expect him to be a really good dad. This means he cares as much as I do. This means he plans activities for the kids.
I want her to keep our house nice, and be really kind to my mom. I also want her to think I'm great.

Now, let's look at the wife's statements. She want her husband to be a better father and plan interesting activities with the kids. Rather than pinning the expectation on him, could you instead include him in your interesting plans? Then you might ask him to do some simple activities with the kids, such as taking them to the park and out for ice cream.

This change in request wouldn't reflect a change of expectation; rather you would be taking leadership in your marriage to fulfill your expectation. You aren't waiting for disappointment to be erased by your partner's magically perfect actions — an impossible expectation — you are helping to create good experiences and closer relationships. Do you see the difference?

Now, let's look at the husband's expectations: He'd like her to keep their home clean and be kind to his mom. Okay, think about a life task, like cleaning, that you want your spouse to participate more in. You need to call a meeting, but only about that one task. Break it down: What does it mean to you to have a clean house? If there is disagreement about your levels of participation, take turns stating desires and expectations. Each one can give a little in order to find some middle ground. Would it be worth it to pay a house cleaner every two weeks and remind the kids to do their chores in exchange for a happy, relaxed relationship?

When it comes to in-laws, everyone has a unique situation. You need to give your partner your top three needs in this area and let him or her know the meaning behind those needs. Here's an example:

I need you to ... call my mom once a week for five minutes.

The reason is that ... when you do this, I feel like we are a team in relation to her. We share the duty of communicating, and she will feel that you like her. Then she won't complain to me and I will feel happier. Your kindness towards her fills me up as well.

I need you to ... come with me to my parent's house every Sunday for brunch.

The reason is that ... this makes me feel loved by you. When you spend time with my family, I know you love my whole self including the little girl I become around my parents and bitchy sister. This makes me happy.

When it comes to your partner telling you, "Honey, you are great!" remind her to tell you this by simply saying, "When you tell me something that you like about me, it makes my whole day." Also, practice telling her she is great and why, and she will want to reciprocate with the same appreciation.

I think you get the idea. Successful communication means being specific and detailed, and it means giving the reason and meaning. These elements make the communications personal, not perfunctory. Such communication also entails asking directly for love with certain words, ways of touch, and emotions. This is one of the easiest ways to transform the whole atmosphere into something you can finally relax into — a higher state of love.

What really counts is how your partner loves you, not how your partner loves your mom or dad or sister or best friend. Maybe you're a giver who loves everyone and maybe your partner just loves you. Loving just you isn't a bad thing, unless you make it into one. You may have told yourself, "My partner has to love who I love." Guess what? You can stop believing that right now. Your partner does not have to love the people you love, just as he or she doesn't have to love the things you love to do!

Let's recalibrate a little: Write down exactly how your partner makes you feel loved. Then tell your partner how she or he makes you feel loved.

Remember that it is natural to reciprocate emotionally. So, if you wish your partner were more this way or that way, embody those ways in relation to him or her. BE the emotion you want to feel. If you want to be appreciated, then show appreciation. Cut out the old excuses: "But I was always appreciative and it didn't work before." That logic won't get you out of taking this action — now. Try appreciating the person right now, the way you know he or she would like to be appreciated. Let yourself be surprised by the experience of sweet appreciation in return. You can fill yourself up with it.

Here's your chance to make it real! Take a moment to think about the next statements, and then fill in the blanks.

My partner makes me feel loved when he/she ...

I will appreciate his/her way of showing me love by appreciating him/her in this way ...

Words:

Actions:

In being able to really feel appreciation and to appreciate your ability to feel it, you become emotionally masterful. You are giving to yourself — and to your partner — on a deep level. Your partner will experience it, feeling your appreciation and then giving it back to you, but even more important, you will be able to fill yourself up with good emotions that you then add into the mix. This exchange works with any positive emotions that you want to be given. Find out how you can give the emotion to another — and really take the time to fully appreciate your emotional state when you give.

CHAPTER 14

Creating Your Mission Statement

One of the biggest traps for a relationship is falling into an insatiable need for appreciation. Instead, we can switch tactics, change the focus from demanding or begging to giving love and feeling love, giving appreciation and feeling that appreciation.

Appreciation is just another form of love, like friendly love, sexy love, supportive love, interesting love, artistic love, sporty love, intellectual love, positive love, or charming love. All of these "types" come from the same place. You can give love in so many ways but what is key is to understand how your partner likes to be loved. If you review the list of examples just offered, you will likely find a few that apply to your partner. And maybe you'll want to add more to fit your specific relationship.

Once identified, you can focus on giving your partner this type (or types) of love. Decide now that every day with your partner, even if you're doing something boring or tedious, you will come from the place of love — in your energy, in your thoughts, and in your actions. This choice — where you are coming from rather than what you are not immediately getting — is key to shifting the entire focus of your relationship. When you are successful in expressing unique forms of love through your energy, your words, and your actions, you can rest assured that you are becoming the ultimate lover.

Let's explore now how to create this powerful love intention on a regular basis. You will place this intention — your mission statement — where you can read it every morning. Your bathroom mirror is one idea. You'll see it in the morning and also in the evening when you are getting ready for bed. Think of it as preparing your spirit to be who you want to be with the most important person in your world. Any love style is welcome! If you're reading and feeling and still brushing your teeth, then fantastic, you are a multitasker! If you close your eyes and feel it in your heart, perfect, you are absorbing! However it works for you, align yourself every day with who you want to be in this relationship. It might sound like this: "I will be loving, passionate, and supportive today. I will charm you, flirt with you, and when I do this, I'm going to feel like the best person in the world, my best self. I love to be loving towards you. I love to be open and adventurous and playful."

Now, take a moment to write down your own sentences. These sentences are for you; they lay out your intention for the day or for the week, they are from you to you, and they remind of who you will be as a lover and partner. Here's your heading ...

Love Intention Statement:

And if you're like 99 percent of us and need reminders during the day too, you can keep a note on your computer or phone or in your pocket. You can even set an alarm to sound two or more times a day to remind you to read your intention.

Every day is a day to recommit to your relationship to your partner. So, practice setting your intention and then start to daily commit to your partner through speaking and living intention. Start with saying it to yourself — and then share it!

CHAPTER 15

Money & Love

It is very often the case that when the couple's conversation turns to finances, spending, or simply what something costs, tension begins to permeate the air. We all have our own rules, meanings, and representations related to money, worth, and value. This sphere can get very tricky when we are sharing our hearts, our lives, and when we are raising kids together. Let's start by looking at the meanings you've created around your partner and money.

DO YOU EVER SAY THINGS TO YOURSELF LIKE ...
If my partner loved me, he or she would _____.

You may have rules for how the person should share, or give, or spend, save, or feel about money.

Most of us have these types of hidden rules about money and love. However, our rules may be so well guarded that we haven't even uncovered their details for ourselves.

If we are really organized, efficient, and practical when it comes to money, saving, and spending, then we often hit our heads against the invisible wall when others are not: "How can my partner not think about the money?" Sometimes we are in such an unknowing and confused space that we tell ourselves that it's best not to even question anything as it will just lead to another blowup. But decades can go by and there is this huge unspeakable third wheel in the relationship. As we ignore it, the wheel grows bigger in the shadows. This third wheel is our confusion and our unspoken questions, the things we steer clear of — differences in spending, giving, earning, and saving. This can have some pretty severe consequences, like not being able to feel good about the money we earn or would like to earn. This avoidance can also present as a difficulty in teaching our children about money because we are afraid to step on our partner's toes by bringing up a painful topic.

On the other hand, there is the couple that just can't stop talking about how different they are in their perspectives. "She is very careful with money, and I am very generous." "We come from two very different worlds when money is concerned. I believe money is for spending and he believes it is for investing." "I don't think she gets how unloving her attitude is about money."

Take a moment now to consider if any of the preceding statements are close to what you think. Then copy the statements down. Now brainstorm your own list of thoughts, beliefs, fears, and hopes regarding: money and love … money and the future … money and self-worth … money and relationships.

My Money Thoughts List:

1.

2.

3.

4.

This can be hard work, but you're doing it with the purpose of making more room in your authentic self for love. Knowing these rules and honoring that we are all different based on upbringing and life experience can free us from conflict or stubbornness and the inability to welcome the other's point of view.

Now let's make a wish list. Look over your Money Thoughts and then jump right into creating this next list — Your Money Wish List. Complete the following stem statements:

I wish money in relationship would....

I wish money in relationship would....

You may wish money would bring you closer, create wonderful experiences together, or be equally valued and shared. Whatever your wish list, add even more now to it, with as many details as you like.

Some examples:

I wish money would be a way for us to celebrate our love.
I wish she liked it when I spent money on myself.
I wish we agreed on an exact amount for our spending budget.

The more we can communicate — at first with ourselves, and then with our partner — in an honest, uplifting, and loving way about our rules, beliefs, and wishes around money, the closer we can be in a loving understanding.

Let's also make a clear goal right now about money and love. This is simply a first goal for the month. Your goal may change, and I hope it does as your relationship and stage of life changes. This first goal applies to the present and is a clear statement that brings you into present time and purpose in your relationship regarding money.

Establishing the First Goal

Some examples:

- My goals regarding money in our relationship (with the intention of greater connection and love) ...

- We give to each other financially every day as an act of love.
- All money that we make is mutual money with no separation between us financially.
- I understand his way with money and he understands my way with money. We respect each other's different spending, saving, and giving styles.

Financial Meetings

One of the best practices you can develop as a couple is to have financial meetings in which the whole point is to address the financial realities of your relationship and your life together. This is a little outline of how to hold such a meeting:

1. Pick a time to meet regularly, whether once a week, every other week, or once a month.

2. Start by taking turns stating your goals for the meeting. Make these goals full of your positive intentions around one area of your marriage such as money, work, parenting, and so on.

3. Allow each other to speak for a specific amount of time, like 10 minutes each. In those 10 minutes express all concerns, hopes, perceived differences, and acknowledge gratitude for the other's listening. Make sure each person has a full turn.

4. Practice asking your partner for more details after he or she is done speaking. Do not correct, state a defense, or offer an opinion. Only ask to understand your partner more.

5. Then after each partner has had a turn, the other should say what he or she understood and what he or she believes would be good changes, goals, or ways of being with money that would help encourage more love, fulfillment, and connection.

Acknowledge where there are differences and make clear that even with differences there is so much love, respect, and honesty — whatever comes to mind that is true and uplifts the relationship.

6. Each partner must decide on one focus point when it comes to money for the next period —one week, two weeks, or month. So you could decide that you will both write down what you spend at the end of each day so you can look at it together at the next meeting. You could decide to go out for an amazing day on the town and practice spending a specified amount, whether 50 or 500 dollars that day on just having a great time together. The point is that you both get to decide and carry out one practice together in the area of money. Whether the practice is to be more generous, to take more risks, be more responsible, careful, or exacting doesn't matter; the strength of this exercise is in listening, communicating what you heard, and respecting the other's plan of action for the period of time between meetings.

7. Give this practice of money meetings about 90 days to see if it brings you closer, allowing for more connection and trust when it comes to money. My guess is that you will experience a positive shift, and that when you understand each other in this area, are willing to really allow for difference, respect, and individuality, the practice will have a tremendous effect on your entire way of being and loving together.

CHAPTER 16

Dating

If anyone tells you that after you get married you don't need to date anymore, I suggest you ask the person if he or she has ever been married. Dating matters! And it has nothing to do with money, or number of children, or intensity of work, or family responsibilities. You need to plan dates. They can be 15 minutes long on Skype or weekend trips away. What matters is that you plan them.

I'm going to give you some examples now because we all need help getting creative and organized, especially when it comes to trying something new. Then, in the next chapter, I will give you some suggestions for magical additions to your dates.

We will look at how to set up dates and how to conclude them. These are two of crucial elements when it comes to dating your partner and rebuilding your love life. So, get ready to start dating again no matter what — I don't care if you've been together for 30 years! Mark and I have been committed to each other for 29 years and we date —and we work on improving our dates all the time. Right now, I'm very excited about creating these sample dates for you because I'll get to experience them too.

If you haven't noticed yet, being a successful, happy, passionate couple takes creativity and brainstorming and planning. Feelings are great, but they need actions and situations to come to life.

Nothing is sadder than the husband who tells us, "I love her so much and I always have," but then we find out they haven't gone on a date for 10 years!

One man thought that the idea of date nights for married people was ridiculous — what mattered to him was saving money and having family time. But he loved his wife deeply and still does. And even though she loves him, she left him and has now found what she needed; she's dating other people, feeling alive, and having lots of new experiences. All these great new and exciting experiences were open to her and her husband, but they just didn't act on the opportunities; they didn't value them.

So if you can relate to this problem, I want you to get ready to date again and to enter an exciting dimension of fun, variety, and fresh experience!

Before going to my examples, I want you to write down some of the best dates you were ever on with your partner —before or after you were married.

Let's do that right now...

Our Best Dates:

1.

2.

3.

4.

Now you've taken the time to recall your best dates. Read through the memories and notice what made them great. Was it a mood? If so, then write "mood" on your list. Was it a visual experience you shared? An auditory experience? Was it a kinesthetic experience? Kinesthetic can include sexual experiences. And if it included sex, what came before or after the encounter? Was it a sex date? Write down "sex date" or "sex during" where appropriate. Keep listing the elements of your best dates.

Do you remember a date in which happiness was the overriding theme? Write it down. Here are more themes to consider: funny dates, committed dates, social dates, adventuresome dates, nature dates, city dates, pet dates, artistic dates. I bet you can come up with at least five more categories. Now make sure to add the location under each one.

What you have now is a list of what you know works for you on dates. Share your list with your partner. Don't share the memories of these dates unless you think they will make your partner happy. Just offer the list of elements within the dates. For example, referring to a Nature Date, you might describe: we walked by the river and it was snowing and I remember feeling how great it was to be in the snow together and how awesome the power of the river was.

Knowing what you like to experience on a date is your special dating magic. Ask your partner what dates were special for him or her. Or take a guess and brainstorm about what the person liked in the past. Some elements might be the same and some may be different now. This is okay!

A friend once told me that the best dates she and her husband ever had happened after they'd finished dry walling or painting a room for their house renovation business. She remembered that great feeling of having worked all day together, and with paint in their hair, wearing their shabby overalls, feeling completely exhausted and looking dirty, they'd open a bottle of wine, sitting on the floor of an empty house, and eating pizza together. For her this was the best. They had shared in hard work and created beauty together, and they felt happy and exhausted. Now they could just relax and enjoy the empty stillness of a home in transition, a place they were making beautiful and warm together.

My friend told this story, clearly longing for that way of working with her husband again. They had a child together, and now she stayed home and built furniture in their garage workshop, but she looked forward to working side-by-side again. For her, working hard together and then relaxing together afterwards made for the best dates.

Some really thrive on sharing in fruitful work and then sharing in the payoff. Others like to create very specific experiences in which daily roles and responsibilities fade away for a while.

CHAPTER 17

Date Ideas

Once you realize the importance of dating your partner, you are halfway there. The next part may need a little priming so the following suggestions will help you create your own list of dating possibilities. You may stray far from my suggestions (or stay quite close) as your own ideas begin to take shape.

1. Blindfold your partner and lay out various foods to taste. Give kisses between bites.

2. Go into nature and bring along what you need to spend several hours there. Be prepared with music, food, blankets, candles, and a book to read aloud.

3. Build a sandcastle together (or a snow castle if you are in a cold climate). You might also consider burying each other in the sand or throwing each other into the water. Shooting water guns could be fun too. Nothing should get in the way of frolicking together.

4. Go to a yoga class or do some yoga together and afterwards talk about the experience. What did you feel when you were in the poses? Sit back-to-back and feel each other's breathing for five minutes. Follow the natural movement from there.

5. Have a picnic in your house. Get lots of fresh fruit, dips, veggies, and finger food, and lay it all out on the floor. Give your partner a sheet to wear. Look online for how to make a toga. Now pretend to be gods and goddesses together. Feed each other, lounge and look at the room from this new perspective, or wear nothing, or stay with your normal clothes — do what works for you.

6. Go to an amusement park without any kids. Bring out your partner's playful side. The long lines give you a chance to talk about the stuff you don't usually explore — a favorite summer memory, a beloved movie, book, childhood friend, or adventure. Try to get to know something new about your partner in every line. Leave your phone in your purse or pocket! No e-mails or text messages.

7. Go to a new coffee house and taste and compare four drinks together. Try holding hands the entire time.

8. Face paint or body paint each other. You can stay home or go out into the world as each other's creation.

9. Go shopping. Let him dress you (buying the clothes is optional). Let her dress you (again, buying the outfit isn't necessary but a picture in the dressing room could be fun).

10. People-watch. Take turns telling each other what you imagine about the strangers you see. Sit close, be funny, be kind, and use your imaginations. You can be anywhere: in a mall, your car, the zoo, a museum, or coffee shop. Wherever there are people, you will have the starting point to imagine together. This date will also give you key information about how your partner sees the world.

11. Cover the bed in rose petals. Be forewarned though: they will stain the sheets (I know from experience!). Ask her to lie down and let you take her picture. Beg her to let you take a picture,

even if she doesn't like pictures. The begging shows her you love how she looks and want to remember the moment with her. If you are a woman planning this date, then surprise him with an image of you on the bed surrounded by rose petals an hour before your date. Planning and setting the stage for romance is a big part of the experience.

12. Get lost. Plan on getting lost together in your own town or city. Drive or bike or walk with the goal of discovery. Give yourself time for surprise and have a conversation with a stranger. Do something nice for someone neither of you knows.

13. Create a surprise by trying something new to both of you. (Only plan this if your partner enjoys surprises.) This could be in the form of an experience or something you are learning together. The sky is the limit: Tai chi, pottery, hot air ballooning, sailing, snow-shoeing, hiking, meditation, a poetry slam, a dance class — anything that is unfamiliar to you.

14. Go to a bookstore and find funny titles together. There are still a few bookstores and goodreads.com will do the trick too. Keep a collection of your favorite titles. The goal is not to crack the book open, only to appreciate the outside. A reverse activity would be to read to each other the final pages of different books and then discuss what the book may be about.

15. Meet at a bar and pretend to be different people on a blind date. Stay in character for the whole "first date." Decide beforehand on the hour you will return to being yourselves. You could dress differently than you usually do and even wear a wig. Be prepared with your character's back story and ideas for conversation, thinking up questions you will ask this new man or woman. You might want to ask about work, family, dating history, and likes and dislikes. Stay in character as long as possible. Enjoy the laughter that follows.

CHAPTER 18

The Kids
(YOURS, THEIRS, SOMEONE ELSE'S)

Whether they are just a twinkle in your eye, never going to happen, or are 7 and 16 or grown adults, children are a part of a couple's life. And often they are in the picture in some way. They could be your best friend's kids or your niece. They may even be far into the future or back in the distant past, but it's time to be open and honest about them.

Do you have some secret wish about how your partner should act or feel towards the kids in your life? If so, then be honest with yourself right now and ask yourself:

Do I have an expectation of how he or she would/should/could act around the kids?

Now ask, is this a fair expectation? Or is it based on personal perspective and history?

What do I know to be unique and special about how my partner does act or feel towards the kids?

QUESTIONS TO ASK YOUR PARTNER ABOUT CHILDREN:

What do you love about each child?

What do you see as each one's strengths?

What in your opinion could they improve?

How could they treat you in a way that you would appreciate?

What could I tell them about our relationship that would make you happy?

How could I be when we are together with them that would make you happy?

To relate well about the kids, you need to be ready to find a middle ground. You need to know that nothing is worse for the kids than a couple's disagreement about them. In other words, you need to decide right now that both of you will find places to compromise.

Let's see what this might mean in action. Maybe you are against Joey playing football and your husband supports it, and although you are against having soda in the house, your husband isn't. You each have to give a little to come to an agreement so that Joey will know the parameters. In this example, perhaps your husband agrees to not allow soda in the house and you agree to let Joey play football. Or, perhaps the two of you decide on a certain amount of soda to be permitted and on the safety precautions that will be taken when playing football. Get the idea?

If you don't have kids yet, but plan to have them, explore these questions with your partner:

How many kids do you think would be ideal?

At what age would you want to have them?

How would you want us to divide and share responsibilities?

Tell me about the people who you think are the best examples as parents.

If you are surprised that your partner never wants kids, then this is the time to ask more about this in a loving way. The goal is only to know more, not to judge. Is he or she afraid of being a terrible parent? Is a difficult childhood behind the feeling? Is it possible that your partner fears responsibility? Is it the desire for a certain lifestyle that precludes children?

You may want to ask if your partner can imagine anything that would change this feeling. Sometimes, people feel very strongly in their 30s that they don't want kids, but come 43, when they are more secure financially and emotionally, that feeling changes. It's good to think about and discuss things before rather than after the fact, to seize the opportunity to be prepared. For example, an important question might be, If having biological children weren't possible, would adoption be okay?

The topic of children should not be left unattended to grow as an unknown. It will ambush you later.

Here are some more questions for your partner about children:
Are there children in your life whom you want me to have a relationship with? Perhaps friends' or siblings' kids? And then explore with your partner if he or she sees a way to be in a relationship with these kids together.

Maybe having a child is not in the plan right now but you'd really like to have a dog or cat? Make this a part of your relationship by brainstorming how you could be animal parents together. Would you be one of those couples with every gadget and toy, or would you enjoy walks with your dog or training classes? Animals give a couple lots of shared experiences that are focused on enjoying the animal and the environments that animals encourage us to visit, such as parks or trails. Animals also encourage socializing with other pet parents.

So, why are you getting all this information from your partner? Because as professionals what we see over and over again is that couples misunderstand each other's plans, wishes, and hopes around parenting. They avoid the important conversations, have secret expectations, and are often surprised by the realities.

And it is simply inaccurate to assume that a happy, successful, passionate relationship develops from agreeing on every detail of raising the kids (or anything else). This simply isn't true. Movement toward a middle ground is essential, yes. It is helpful to be flexible and communicate well, trying to understand the other's point of view.

Can you be radically different and not sacrifice in love? Yes! Can you feel that although this part of your relationship isn't the strongest, it doesn't mean that your marriage is doomed? It just means that co-parenting is more challenging — and demands more creativity, perhaps — than the other parts of the relationship. Remember Chapter 8, the chapter on having many marriages within one marriage? It's one of those moments to pay close attention to the strengths of your marriage, the easier parts (marriages) that surround this more challenging one.

You can also tell your kids what is strong in your marriage by showing them how much you love each other. When you do this — and I don't care if your children are toddlers or adults, or are someone else's kids — you help them at the most profound level to know that a loving, successful, passionate marriage is possible for them too. You let them know by virtue of being witness to a relationship that isn't perfectly in lockstep all of the time but still is full of life, full of joy, full of love.

Truthfully, the more problems that you resolve and love your way through, the more your kids know that they can be successful in love too. So, go for it — with public displays of affection, sweet nicknames, regular dates, and trips alone together. And if you're lucky enough to hear your kids say, "Dad just wants to be with you, Mom" or "Mom cares more about her trip with you than my dance recital," you should say to yourself, "I did it! My kids know I'm in love."

You can find a thousand ways to reassure them of your devotion and love for them too. Sometimes they may think that you love your partner more than you love them, but you can show them that it's just a different type of love and that they will enjoy this type of romantic love one day too.

CHAPTER 19

Passion & Chemistry

THE ART OF DESIRE

Why did we make you wait so long for this topic? A simple explanation: trust. I'm not talking about trusting this book. I'm talking about trust in your relationship. We want you to feel a deep trust with your lover before you start to turn up the heat in the bedroom.

Some of you may be overachievers, and you've already experienced better sex and intimacy. That's excellent. Still, you may wonder at some point how can we feel more passion or get a partner to be more passionate. The foundation is trust. When a woman feels safe and secure, she can let go and experience deeper passion. When a guy trusts his partner, he can show up in a new way, a more assertive directed way, which will be a spark for both. Building masculine presence will be explored in the next chapter.

To help you understand more about your own passion and trust cycle, I will tell you a few great stories of couples we've coached.

MEET THE CHARLESTONS

The Charlestons did just one thing to create a huge shift in the first three weeks of relationship coaching. Every morning, he would go to her. While she was still asleep, he would sing to her for just a few minutes. Through song, he'd tell her how much he loved her and what he appreciated about her. Sometimes, he'd just hold her and impart the feeling of his love. Before this time, his wife doubted his devotion, but now, based on this seemingly small gesture, she felt nurtured and safe. They had created this ritual together, and, more important, he took action and made sure he did it every day. What happened for her was miraculous. She wanted him again. And she wanted to make love with him. This change occurred despite many years of her struggling with loss, depression, and distrust.

So, if you don't have one yet, a ritual you do every day is a fantastic first step in creating passion. Add three minutes to each day when you express to your partner your huge love and what you notice that's amazing about him or her. Remember, the ritual doesn't have to lead to sex; what you're doing is building the foundation so that passion can be sparked and then ignited.

Meet Lisa and Matthew

Now, let's talk about a radically different type of couple. Lisa is 43 and Mathew is 60. This couple was in a committed 10-year relationship but felt something was missing. It turned out that Lisa hadn't been able to commit to getting married, even though they had lived together for 10 years and both felt a lot of love for each other. She explained how she knew for sure that he loved her. She felt safe, protected, even adored, but something stopped her from wanting to show him affection. She had no problem having sex, but affectionate kissing and intimacy were challenging for her. It was very hard for her to pinpoint what was keeping her from feeling and expressing this type of affection, and from wanting to get married.

She shared with me the story of her life in romantic relationships. We went through the story of each relationship. All together, she had had six meaningful relationships. And what we discovered was that the lovers who she'd had a lot of chemistry with weren't the guys any rational woman would want to marry.

These men weren't exactly bad boys; one was a fantastic lover and friend, but the problem was that he was also a fantastic lover and friend to many women at once, usually three at a time. He didn't keep this from her, and their encounters were still some of the best intimate memories of her life. Why? What was revealed as she told the story was that the total focus on the moment, maybe the excitement of not owning his love, and his ability to completely guide the lovemaking, made her feel fantastic.

Now, the other man she had this type of intense connection with was very different from her, from a different kind of family and with different priorities, but when he was with her he was really with her. She didn't know if it would last, since they were so different, and there were no false promises.

Coaching Lisa reminded me just how different we are as people, whether we are men or women. There is often this idea that a woman needs certainty and predictability to feel trust and to get turned on. It's a myth. Many people need something else to feel passion — to feel a sense of frozen time, no future, no promises, just total presence in the living moment. Lisa needed a bit of uncertainty to feel the chemistry and passion with a lover. She also needed the man to really take charge of the lovemaking, to tell her what to do in bed in order for her to feel perfect for him in that moment, and that he will take her where she needs to go to experience passion.

Many of us are used to the idea of being equal as lovers, just like in the rest of life: I do this and then you do this. And while taking turns can be fun when making love, for some people the most chemistry and passion happens when one partner, the more feminine partner (not necessarily a woman), is taken through an experience without having to do anything. She trusts her man to tell her when he wants something and then she's happy to give it. Get the difference? This isn't an equal is better situation. Now, of course, it's always fun to experiment, and women should feel they can take the lead and guide the lovemaking if that's what turns them on. Some couples like to make sex a game, and others like to forget all about thinking and go with instinct. Whatever your style, the goal is to enjoy yourself. It can be helpful to ask this question but not to answer it. Rather, allow the sex to be the answer: "What would make our sex even better?"

What I've found in talking to hundreds of women is that they are sometimes shy about telling their men to take over. And the guys are sometimes working off manufactured examples in movies or in pornography of what a turned-on woman is like. If they've spent a lot of time in manufactured sexual imagery, they may approach their real love-making with preconceived ideas of what she should do or how she should be in bed.

I'm going to be very direct and clear now. If you or your partner is addicted to pornography, then it could be hurting your sex life. If you and he enjoy sexual movies or porn together and it adds to your sex life, fantastic. But get educated if you're the guy, and then ask her how she feels about you watching porn. Is there porn she likes? Is she curious? If you're a woman, tell him honestly how you feel about it. Be specific. For some women, there are types of porn that are more "okay" than others. It is really fine to have rules here, just not hidden ones. What is important is being very clear and making sure that you value the relationship more than the porn habit.

Both partners need to understand how watching porn benefits or detracts from the relationship. There is no one answer for every couple, but I do like to ask each individual to consider the following: Is my sexual relationship with the man or woman I love more important or less important than my habit of watching porn? Since the answer is usually that the sexual relationship is more important, it might be time to take action, listen to your partner, and create new habits in bed with the real-life lover you have. Figure him or her out and do not rely on movies to inform you about what is a turn-on or turn-off in bed. Ask lots of questions to understand your partner. Find out what you do and what you don't do that he or she likes. Ask about fantasies. Then try different things and ask for feedback. Your lover will feel your caring and devotion as you learn more about his or her desires.

It can be a revelation to share the urge you have to have sex in the shower. Take a risk and let your lover know details: you like oral sex every time you make love or maybe you don't enjoy oral sex ever. I find that detailed information that comes from a loving passionate place almost always improves the chemistry. And yet this level of frankness does require a great deal of courage. Even to admit you want to try something new but are scared, or that you have no idea how to engage in a certain type of sex, can be challenging. But it's usually worth taking on the challenge! Chances are there is something new that is worth exploring in the bedroom. Part of building your love to its ultimate potential is really owning this role in your life.

Be a researcher. Buy books that explain sexual techniques. Ask questions of your partner. Be ready to experiment. Be ready to laugh when something doesn't work. Let all of you show up, and take a risk or two!

CHAPTER 20

Presence: The Man Inside

What is presence?
Well, I'm talking about the energy that can be present, consistent, and steady. I am talking about a level of energy that shows — more than tells — that your love is here to stay. To be a present man is to be a rock. Now, here's the thing: Depending on the woman you're with, the rock can't be silent. The rock may need to talk and repeat and reassure about how much you love her. This rock is an energy, not an entity. Sometimes, the man has to show his emotions through his eyes and through his energetic being, emanating his love and how solid he is.

Now, I am talking directly to the men: I want you to name this man in you, this person I know you are, who can give to your woman a solid, steady love, the type of love that she needs. Think of a name for this man in you, this rock, this being present. Write the name down.

Now, ask yourself what your partner craves to hear, and how, as a solid source of love, you are going to express it to her. Through words, through touch, through looks, through presence? Take a moment to write some notes about who this man is inside of you and what he will do or say.

When I am being a present partner I say these types of things ...

At times I get triggered and hide. These are my triggers …

I can overcome my triggers by reminding myself of these internal strengths …

I can overcome my triggers by focusing on what is more important, the purpose of my love …

When she is upset, I can say this to show my presence …

This presence within you is always there, it is you, and can be called into action any time. Sometimes, your partner may need this steady presence and sometimes you may need it. Make sure you know how to call this part of you into leadership by practicing every day for a week. It's simple, just focus on this presence within for a few minutes and then ask it if has any information for you and write down what it says.

CHAPTER 21

Boy and Man

Our work with couples has shown that the transition between being a boy and being a man is really important for men to be aware of in themselves.

Following are some examples of where this transition often causes trouble for the heterosexual couple:

A husband and wife go out for dinner, have a great time, and on their drive home, she tells him about a woman who was treated unfairly. He makes a joke about the woman but his wife feels the joke is immature, disrespectful, and dismissive, and they get into a fight. She was seriously bringing up an issue and the man has just acted from the place of the little obnoxious boy inside (not the lovable one). As a woman, it is helpful to recognize that the obnoxious boy is not your favorite part of him, and that you are very lucky that he doesn't usually act like that 12-year-old. If you are a guy, you might catch yourself being that young kid and say out loud, "Hey, who was that?" Being the obnoxious 12-year-old is great fun when you're with the guys or watching a silly movie, but not always on a date with your wife.

Some women love the boy inside the man. They will let you know by laughing and joking to bring this part of you out more often. If this is an important part of you and it bothers your partner, find ways to be playful and funny that are simultaneously loving and inclusive. This could mean buying toys and playing games or going on adventures together. It certainly means being sensitive to when your wife is being serious and requires a respectful response.

Here's another example of the boy who comes out in a way that chips away at the passion in the relationship. When a husband and wife both enjoy their kids but the husband acts like he's one of them, and the wife then feels like she has to be everybody's mom. It can be tough to have to be the warrior all the time at home to get things done.

Sometimes this dynamic comes into play when we are triggered by our partner. Imagine this scenario: whenever the woman gets upset, her boyfriend gets upset too and goes for a walk. He wanders around aimlessly for hours, trying to figure out how he feels. He has regressed emotionally and is very confused, like a lost boy. If this happens to you (whether you are a man or a woman), it is helpful to ask yourself, "What age am I right now?"

On these occasions when the man shifts suddenly into being a boy, and it's a total surprise for the woman, it's an ambush. Right when she needed him to be a man, he switched to being a boy and let go of his protective and supportive role. So it's very important to understand this difference. Again, I am speaking to the men: Notice when this happens to you, and remind yourself, "What is my new name?" Call that present rock-man into being and use his strength to communicate.

Let's consider some of the differences between boys and men. Of course, these are generalizations and archetypes, but I think they'll help you with a key distinction. Think of the man as the strong solid protective source of love who is immovable in his attention but also expressive, kind, and loving.

On the other hand, if you think about mindset of a boy, say between the ages of 10 and 13 years old, you can imagine (or recall) the type of humor that he engaged in. He's obsessed with not being a man. Where a man is present, the boy jokes about escaping.

Where a man shows responsibility and commitment, the boy laughs about dodging commitment, shirking responsibility, and being the joker. Where a man is directed and self-reflective, the boy is busy trying to get a rise out of other people.

Think about the movies that are made for boys — think about all those movies that joke about being a man, make everything ridiculous, and laugh about sex and farting and anything to do with the body. The characters are self-deprecating and insulting to others. Think about the locker room banter about sex, about women, when actually they know nothing about women. This is the world of a boy. Boys are scared of being men, so they joke about it. They're unfamiliar with women, likely afraid, so they joke about them too.

And, of course, there are also some great things about being a boy! They can be a lot of fun. They don't take anything too seriously. They avoid responsibility so they're happy to run away from the world with you. They like to wander around and get lost. Think of Johnny Depp's role as the pirate, the adult boy. He's interesting, he's fun, but he's there for himself, not to take care of others.

Sometimes a man is so diligent and responsible that he loses the playful boy in him. Most women want to be with a man who knows how to smile and say, screw it all, let's run away from the world for a couple hours, days, or weeks. They want the man to have access to the boy — just not to rely on him!

There's a balance to be struck. You don't want to be the boring, super responsible man all the time, but you also don't want to morph into a boy just when your woman needs you. Finding a balance means knowing yourself.

Make the distinction:

Think about when you tend to act in accord with these images. Write down the situation in which it is likely to happen:

A present man (give him a name):
An obnoxious boy:

A fun romantic boy:

For women —
Write down when you enjoy the boy in your man:
Write down when you most need him to be really present, a rock:

CHAPTER 22

Polarity

Each of us contains both masculine and feminine energies. These energies fluctuate to give us a sense of polarity and interest — a state of being awake and alert to our humanness. This polarity also wakes us up and shows us we are interested in the body, in passion, and in closeness to our mates. I believe that each person has his or her own definition of what it means to be masculine and what it means to be feminine; it is your true meaning that is most important.

I have also found that sharing my definition has helped some people recognize the parts of themselves that can be described as either masculine or feminine.

The masculine can be seen as directed, taking charge, and showing others where it is possible to go. As a woman, you may feel this very strongly while also feeling very in touch with your essence as a mother. A mother takes her children in the right direction, guiding and teaching them. She holds a strong space for them to play and explore safely within the expression of her love, commitment, and warmth. She is experiencing her own masculine energy in her role as leader and mother.

To experience *feminine energy*, I like to use the example of being so honest, so courageous, and so open to the world that you have no fear. This fearlessness can feel vulnerable in the best of ways. It allows for a very deep connection without needing to protect or guard against emotions.

Then there is the play between the masculine and feminine inside all of us. You can experience your own inner polarity. Have you ever worked very hard, using your intense focus and mental energies, pushing yourself to achieve, or pass a test, clean the house, or meet a deadline? When the task is over, you crash. You need to stop and just be. You feel vulnerable, full of emotions, and you need to rest, regroup, gather yourself, and nurture yourself, allowing emotions to flow freely through you.

This is different from the common description of the sexy kind of polarity, the opposite forces attracting and igniting inside of us. The focus and intensity gives way to openness and vulnerability — body, mind, spirit.

Some of us enjoy lots of polarity all the time. This is a sign that variety is an important need. You may feel both masculine and feminine in this way during the course of an hour or even just 5 minutes.

Others can't stand these dramatic swings, so they tend to keep life simple. All of us create patterns that keep us balanced. We wish to stay close to center. This is particularly strong in certain people, and they tend to value routine and certainty.

Neither preference can be seen as being right or wrong — it is simply an aspect of who we are. One person will say, "I'm strong because I stay steady. I balance myself daily, even hourly, so that I can be open, receptive, directed, and focused." Another says, "I love to give one area of my life everything I've got. I work like crazy during the week, with complete focus, always striving to be the best. But then when Friday comes, I unwind totally; I'm a different woman. I put on different clothes, I even smile differently, and the soft, warm little girl in me gets to play."

Both these women are feminine and both have mastered the art of polarity within themselves.

If you choose a man whose energy supports your rhythm, a man who knows his own patterns and knows how to dance with your energies, you both will experience tremendous passion and love. All that you have done so far through this book has supported this energy inside of you. The actions you take to understand and love your man supports his ability to be present and playful with your feminine energy.

However, sometimes women struggle with their inner polarity. When a woman experiences her own rhythms but is unaware and undereducated about her emotions, she may feel and act in ways that she doesn't understand. She blows up at her family because she can't drop the directed, focused, warrior mentality of her job persona. She is on alert constantly. The only way she may be able to enter a different state is through unhealthy substances that induce her relaxation response.

It may occur to you that this type of pattern resembles that of a tough hard-working lawyer or executive. Frankly, women who are not in these fields but are moms sometimes have to be warriors too. Even when they are overflowing with estrogen and baby hormones and staying home to nurture their children, they are in the warrior — their masculine — mode. They find themselves feeling responsible for so many details of family, children, and house. They need to be strong. They need to enforce schedules and rules. They manage through calling on their warrior energy.

If this describes some of what you've experienced, you aren't alone. Many women struggle with their need to be strong and direct. If you have discovered that you are a little burned out or need more openness, you might be wondering how you can bring this natural polarity back into your being and into your relationship. If you're a mother, you know it's a more than full-time job, and that you are on call 24/7. Even at night, when the baby wakes up, you're on alert. Worry becomes your constant partner. What if the baby chokes on her food? What if a burglar breaks into the house? The warrior's worries may take over, which makes it hard to switch out of this state of readiness and move into a space of openness and ease.

When I talk with women who are in this phase of life, they usually report that this part of them feels tired and wants a break.

Perhaps you recognize this in yourself. You may feel more than ready to put down your heavy armor and go on vacation. To do this, you will need to trust the other parts of yourself, your archetype sisters, which represent the creative forces in you, the forces that instigate magic, the part of you that enjoys the moment and wants your partner to take the lead so you can rest and enjoy.

What Are Your Archetypes?

Now I am speaking to the women ...

Take a moment to make a list of the different parts of yourself. Are there specific personalities inside you that surface at various times of the day or when engaged in a certain activity? In Passion Patterns, we call these your archetypes, and two of the most common ones in women are the "warrior" and the "lover," or as I like to call her, the goddess. There is also the "magician," who is creative and magical, and the "sovereign," who sees it all and finds solutions with ease. Sometimes there is a "rebel" or a "healer."

Explore the archetypes in you and ask them questions. Does someone need a break or is someone in need of more support from her sisters?

Questions to ask your archetypes to glean the benefit of their wisdom and advice.

How can I let you out more often?

What would you like to tell me?

Is there something in my regular life that can serve to remind me of your presence within me?

As you learn to work with your archetypes you may find the need for a specific energy arises whether at work, at home, when you have stress, or during sex. Since you now know your archetypes, you can draw forth their spirit and wisdom by calling them into action when you need them. In practicing these energies and speaking to them you are inviting them into greater presence in your life. I suggest spending a few minutes a day allowing yourself to think about them and to ask the questions we've laid out for you. In just a week you will know these energies within you in a very deep and profound way.

Archetypes may be female or male or animal or ethereal. There also may be several types of lover or warrior. Be open for what is real to you. You will be gaining creativity, power, and communication with your core integrated self as you explore these different parts of self. Men can use this same process of speaking and getting to know their archetypes. Couples may want to share this experience with each other or keep it as private wisdom. Trust yourself to decide what is needed and allow this to evolve as you deepen the relationship with these parts of self.

CHAPTER 23

Warrior & Goddess

Let's focus on the warrior and the goddess in you. How do you honor the two sides, the energies of the warrior and the energies of the goddess inside of you?

Our most powerful coach is inside of us. We know ourselves, we've shared our own past, we hold our dreams inside our hearts, and we experience our lives in a way no one else can truly understand.

The warrior: If you'd like to ask the different parts of yourself for advice and help, you can start by feeling the energy and power of the warrior inside of you.

How does she stand? Envision her stance and then take a moment to physically stand like her.

A warrior likes to tell it how it is. So let's ask your warrior some direct questions:

How do you feel in your body as warrior?

How do you feel emotionally?

What is your most important job?

What are you protecting?

Are you planning anything special this week?

Are there any pending or past confrontations that have been on your mind?

The goddess: Now let's meet your goddess. Allow yourself to make contact with her energy and power.

How do you stand or sit or lie down as the goddess? (Remember, you can move around — you are a goddess.)

Goddess, what part of your skin, hair, or body feels nice to you? (Go ahead and feel that part of yourself.)

Is there a physical action you like to take or a posture you hold as the goddess? (Perhaps it is to touch her hair, or to roll her shoulders back and down, lifting her chest and opening up.)

Do you hold your head a little differently as the goddess? Stand up if you are sitting or lying down. Notice how you stand.

What would you like to ask her? Ask the goddess your question. Ask it until you have an answer.

Now, I would like you to ask her something very important and write down the answer your are given. Goddess, how can I enter this feeling state more often?

Is there something you can you tell yourself to do that will remind you of this experience as the goddess?

The goddess is a central figure, here some additional questions for her:
What phrase should I say so you know that I need you to be with me?

Is there anything you are now ready to do that you want me to know about?

Is there anything you as the goddess would like to say to the warrior?

Dialogue between the goddess and warrior:

Now let your goddess speak to your warrior. You can begin with: "Warrior, I appreciate how much you take care of me. Now I need the goddess to speak with you. Goddess, go ahead and tell the warrior what you need."

Write it all down!

Now, take the stance of your warrior. "Warrior what do you need to let the goddess know?"
"Warrior what can you do to help the goddess?"

Write down the responses, and then thank your warrior.

Now take a deep breath and allow the goddess to enter again. "Hello goddess."
"What do you need me to do so that I may feel your energy in me?"

Write down what came, and thank your goddess.

Time to come back to the whole:
Shake it out now. Take a deep breath and exhale fully. I'd like you to stretch for a moment in order to return to yourself. You are an amazing woman who is both the warrior and the goddess (and more). You now know you can call your energies forward when you need them.

You have this essential polarity inside of you and it's available whenever you want to add polarity to your relationship. Remember what the goddess asked you to do to feel her energy. She is you and she is there for you. So is your warrior. Your warrior will always protect you. Of course, from time to time, she may become tired and grouchy and lack the emotional insight to tell you that she needs a break. You will feel her energy take over. This is because it's her job to protect you. You can let her know she needs a holiday, and that it is permitted for her to take one. All warriors need rest and nourishment.

Remember, when you are the goddess, you are letting your warrior relax. She will be a smarter and braver warrior in the future as a result. Each of us contains special archetypes, and in honoring them we not only integrate our authentic self we create a new force in our relationship. As this force comes to life, we know ourselves better and we take the actions needed for deepening our love.

CHAPTER 24

Resistance to Love

THE FINAL FRONTIER

Using Passion Patterns in your marriage should allow you to feel a lot more connected. So why do couples that are growing and experiencing love more often sometimes seem to back pedal? It's not useful to jump to a worst-case scenario, such as you aren't meant to be together or that you are too different to work things out. Even when communication has improved, and your emotions are mostly positive, there can still be a shadow lurking nearby that seems to be very powerful and even mysterious. I call this force "resistance." Resistance shows up just when you are thinking, "I've got this, I know my priorities, I am skillful and passionate." Then, like a tornado, resistance swoops in and fills you with doubt.

The self-doubt and relationship-doubt may be veiled in logic and concurrent feelings, and then solidified by conversations you have. Resistance is believable and persistent. Why? Because it is working to protect you from future hurt or risk. One thing I've learned repeatedly in my own marriage and from the hundreds of marriages that I've helped heal is that resistance only shows up when there is great love. So, don't worry or panic. Instead, learn the signs of resistance. And like an old friend who surprises you for a visit, invite resistance in, get to know this guest now.

Resistance changes over time. As love deepens, resistance often shows up. Think of resistance as a protective part. The following examples of resistance — and the steps to handle resistance when it is trying to interfere with your love and joy — will be helpful.

Resistance of the Mind

When resistance shows up as thoughts and loops of memory there is a tendency to believe the mind. After all, we have spent a long time building our ability to think, use reason, learn, and remember. Resistance uses these abilities to create persistent doubts and fears. Here are some examples of how such doubts and fears may sound internally.

"He loves me but will never really value me."

"I think she is the one, but if she really were wouldn't I be more certain?"

"If I can't understand his rationale, we must be too different to make it work."

"I keep replaying every comment that has hurt me, which means my mind wants me to end things."

Your thoughts may become more intricate and detailed and dramatic. Sometimes, resistance shows up as a long list that we keep adding to. Some of you know a lot about such lists. Your list might be labeled with plusses and minuses or pros and cons or some other type of comparison that supports inaction and promotes that hesitation to feel love.

A great indication that our resistance is of the "thinking type" is when the heart feels differently. An inner battle ensues. Another great hint is when we recognize a pattern in our thoughts, a tendency to always analyze or compare until it becomes difficult to feel. At times we all do this. However, when you have just improved your love relationship and are starting to feel new levels of connection and closeness and then suddenly experience this rerouting in your thoughts, you can bet that resistance is paying you a visit. This resistance wants you to doubt, question, and ultimately guard yourself against hurt.

When Resistance Becomes Feelings

After a thought is fueled by resistance, a strong emotion will often come in to offer back-up. Emotions may also present on their own, getting reinforcement from thoughts. And emotions can come in like a tornado all at once in a swirling chaos of feeling and thinking. As in the tornado, the effect can be devastating.

Feelings of longing, sadness, desperation, regret, hopelessness, fear, passion and anger may accompany it. Emotions serve as warning signals. And if we really want a happy passionate relationship, resistance will likely use emotions to attempt to maintain the status quo. In other words, the more you want something, the greater the chance that resistance will appear.

Again, think of resistance as protective — but it is protection that protects against all shifts in the landscape, even positive ones! You can assure resistance of your resolve to embrace greater joy and connection.

Extroverted Resistance

There is also a form of resistance that is quite outgoing. When this form shows up, you don't necessarily know why you are doing what you are doing. Have you ever spent the evening cleaning when you wish you had asked your partner to make love? Resistance. And you didn't even realize why you were manically dusting, organizing the closet, and folding the laundry.

Or, maybe you start to notice a wandering eye — your own. You notice everyone who could possibly replace your lover. Or, worse, you feel drawn to a particular person and even act on it just when things were going really well.

You might say something to a friend that is a cutting criticism of your relationship and then wonder where the sentiment came from. Resistance can feel like a kettle blowing out steam. Just when the relationship has heated up and the love is flowing, you are suddenly doing, saying, thinking, or feeling all the junk that can put your love in jeopardy.

Three Steps to Counter Resistance

You can freeze resistance in its tracks and send it packing. Pause. Take hold. Use the following strategies!

- Third Perspective
- Exploration with Questions
- Applying Healing Actions

1. Developing the Third Perspective

Whenever you catch resistance at work, you are entering the third perspective and this is a fantastic place to be. Before doing anything else, celebrate your ability to see resistance for what it is: a force that comes from the deep need to protect yourself from failure, hurt, and fear.

When you see that resistance is taking over, you are breaking the cycle through noticing. Now you have taken the necessary pause to explore within. You can ask yourself some questions and also apply a helpful visualization metaphor. A visualization might be to see resistance as a storm blowing in from the West. Then imagine the sun peeking through the clouds, as the wind diminishes and a sense of calm permeates the air.

2. Exploring with Questions

The central question: "What is underneath this thought, feeling, or action?"

The next questions might include:

"Does this thought, feeling, or action serve my relationship purpose or is it attempting to derail me from creating more love in my life?"

"Have I been here before? Is this a familiar pattern from my past?"

"Am I borrowing someone else's beliefs, emotions, or arguments?"

"Can I expand my love right now and push this resistance out of my experience?"

"Can I remember my desire for love, closeness, connection and create a new state right now?"

"Is there an image of a fearless me that will empower me in this moment?"

Do I have a strong value that is more important to me than this temporary thought, emotions or experience?

3. Applying Healing Actions

After exploring through questions (and, keep in mind that the same one question can work for you every time), you can take action. Actions take the form of new thoughts, experiences, or memories, which build up your love power. Actions are helped by physiological changes in posture and breathing as well as changes in location. This is often why people go get a snack when they are bored or frustrated. However, we don't need to grab a bag of potato chips, we can take an action that empowers our love.

Examples of Actions:

Remember a time that you felt full of love, victory, caring, or hope.

Remind yourself of your relationship mission and purpose.

Do something that empowers your sense of self-appreciation and connection with self, the world, and your partner.

The force of love is always more powerful than the need for resistance. As soon as we apply any form of love, resistance can melt away, irrelevant. After all, resistance arrived full of fear and a desire to protect. Your love, acceptance, strength, and willingness to get to the heart of your desire is the essential antidote.

As you become an expert in the subject of your own resistance, this part of you no longer will feel the need to visit. Others will notice your sense of relationship purpose. Your partner will feel your commitment at a new level and be ready to fully embrace your love.

Closing this Book — Opening to What's Next

Congratulations! If you have read, thought about, written down, and taken action on the explorations in this book, you have likely seen positive changes in your relationship already. Good work! It's not easy to take action, and you and your partner deserve a lot of credit for making the time and investing the energy in your relationship, especially when that means opening up and being vulnerable.

Keep in mind that the book is meant to be an ongoing resource. Once you have read it cover-to-cover, you may want to go back to certain sections, perhaps work on questions you had initially skimmed or update exercises. You may have gone through the book by yourself and now feel the time is right to sit with your partner and get his or her perspectives. You may even want to form a small group to explore the ideas together.

In any case, I hope that you'll continue to use — and expand upon — the strategies in this book going forward. Borrowing from the great Mahatma Gandhi: My premise is that each of us needs to be the change we wish to see in our world.

My message to you is simple ...

As you grow in your ability to appreciate, prioritize, communicate, and be creative in your relationship, love naturally becomes happier!